What they're saying about Once Upo[illegible] and the 1951 U. S. Amateur:

If you love golf and golf history, Robin McCool's detailed account of the 1951 U.S. Amateur at Saucon Valley, Once Upon a September is a must read. Filled with fascinating biographical information on many of the competitors, this is a book that you simply cannot put down.

Gene Mattare, *Director of Golf/General Manager*
Saucon Valley Country Club

Robin McCool isn't just a fine golfer. He's a great storyteller of golf. Once Upon a September revives the legend of Billy Maxwell, Eugene Grace and the 1951 U.S. Amateur, when the game was smaller, yet somehow bigger, than it is today.

Mark Wogenrich
The Morning Call

Robin McCool's in-depth account of Billy Maxwell's victory in the 1951 U.S. Amateur at Saucon Valley breaks new ground in the game's history by capturing a snapshot of golf's landscape in the era immediately following World War II. McCool is able to deliver a compelling profile of one of golf's most underappreciated players through his unique perspective as one of the Lehigh Valley's greatest amateur players.

Mike Davis
Executive Director, USGA

I got to know Billy Maxwell during our collegiate golf days and have always considered him a good friend and fine player. His victory in the 1951 Amateur was certainly no surprise. It's nice that it is documented in this book.

Arnold Palmer

"Saucon Valley is hard to write about
because there's not just one feature to
lead off with – everything's outstanding."

Chick Evans
August, 1951

ONCE UPON A SEPTEMBER

ONCE UPON A SEPTEMBER

Saucon Valley and the 1951 U.S. Amateur

Robin McCool

Library of Congress Control Number: 2015919783

ISBN:	Hardcover	978-1-5144-3050-7
	Softcover	978-1-5144-3049-1
	eBook	978-1-5144-3048-4

Print information available on the last page.

Rev. date: 03/21/2016

To order additional copies of this book, contact:
Xlibris
1-888-795-4274
www.Xlibris.com
Orders@Xlibris.com
727840

Contents

Foreword

This book wonderfully chronicles a noteworthy event in Saucon Valley Country Club's history, introducing it to a national audience by hosting its first USGA championship. Saucon Valley has gone on to host seven USGA national championships since, the most in Pennsylvania after Merion and Oakmont. I cannot think of a more appropriate author to write about this USGA championship playing experience. Robin McCool has won more golf championship titles at Saucon Valley than any other golfer in its esteemed history. His golf resume is extensive and truly amazing. In addition, he has served as an Executive Committee member for the Golf Association of Philadelphia for nine years, Junior Golf Chair, Green Committee Chair, and various other committees at Saucon Valley over many years.

While reading this book, my mind wandered back to the fact that this national championship started an amazing and important era at Saucon Valley. Soon after this event club leadership showed amazing vision, and determination, by expanding the Club's grounds and facilities. The inside nine of the Grace course opened in 1953, followed by the outside nine of Grace, Villa Pazzetti, and the six hole practice course in 1957. With Weyhill opening for play a decade later, Saucon

Valley, now totaled 60 pristine holes of golf and a club facility unequalled anywhere in the U.S. or world.

The Club's early leaders were my inspiration when I began a strong push for reinvestment in the Club just after the turn of the 21st century. I have always been a firm believer that we have an obligation to reinvest in Club facilities in order to always offer excellence to our members and their guests. An exceptional private club can't live and thrive on past accomplishments---a club must always be looking forward to be strong and relevant. Saucon Valley Country Club is an American jewel and could never be built again. Aggressively and responsibly reinvesting over $30 million in capital improvements over the past 10 years through course renovations, etc., Saucon Valley has seen a resurgence of pride and utilization during a time when many private clubs have struggled.

Eugene Grace was a visionary and strong supporter of amateur golf. He was part of a group of gentlemen who founded Saucon Valley in addition to being a founding member of the Augusta National Golf Club. He obviously ran a very successful steel company that gave him financial resources to help accomplish these things, but he still had to respect and admire the great game of golf to invest time, talent, and treasure in it. I, and many others, will be forever thankful for that. It is wonderful to read books like this about events in the 1950's and 60's and all those individuals that came before us helping to build and give back to the game of golf.

I must admit, prior to this book, I had never read much about Billy Maxwell, and had no idea he eventually became a golf professional and played on a Ryder Cup team. Billy Maxwell is yet another example of a thoughtful person who gave back to the game he loved. This story has inspired me to learn more about all the past champions of USGA championships held at

Saucon Valley. These national champions and Saucon Valley Country Club will forever share a special bond.

In closing, I would like to say that Robin McCool exemplifies all the gentlemanly aspects of the game of golf and continues to give back to the game in many ways, but specifically by writing this excellent history of the 1951 U.S. Amateur Championship. I hope you enjoy reading about this seminal event as much as I did.

Thank you, Robin, for continuing to give to the game of golf!

Andrew F.S. Warner, President
Saucon Valley Country Club, 2010 -2015

Acknowledgments

Many people contributed to the making of this book. Billy Maxwell, and daughter Melanie Maxwell Bevill are at the top of this list. My personal interview with Billy Maxwell is the focal point of this entire work. Research into the many interesting personalities and events of the 1951 U.S. Amateur at Saucon Valley Country Club provided a great deal of material, but eventually everything circles back to the heart of this book --- Billy Maxwell. The Maxwell family's cooperation made this book possible.

A special mention of appreciation goes to Matt Borocz, Director of Golf at TPC Sawgrass, and his staff for their very generous hospitality during my trip to Jacksonville, Florida to meet with the Maxwells.

Special thanks to dear friends Chick and Cheryl Kozloff for hosting me during my time in Florida.

My sincere appreciation goes to immediate past president of Saucon Valley Country Club, Andrew Warner, for his wonderful Foreword. Many share Andy's love of Saucon Valley, but few have given back so much. Andy's appreciation for the history of our Club is only matched by his vision for its future.

The unconditional support of Gene Mattare, Saucon Valley Country Club's Director of Golf and General Manager, is greatly appreciated. Gene was there for me from the beginning and was always available whenever I needed help or advice. Likewise, my sincere appreciation goes to Saucon Valley Country Club for granting me unlimited access to Club archives and for permission to use video archives for the companion piece to the book.

Good friend, and published golf author, William Godfrey, provided the initial information and motivation necessary for me to undertake this project. Ever since William allowed me to participate in the research and write the Foreword to his book, *Maryvale Golf Course, The First 50 Years*, a flame of inspiration kindled within me.

Several librarians assisted with my research. Nancy Stulack, Lyle Slovick, and Victoria Student of the USGA Library were very helpful. Bess King and Steven Firgko of the E. W. Fairchild-Martindale Library at Lehigh University also helped.

Many others assisted along the way. David Staebler, USGA Director of Rules Education, and a longtime friend, made himself available to answer any of my questions and assist with research whenever asked.

Bernie Loehr, recently retired USGA Director of Amateur Status, was extremely helpful with research pertinent to Chapter 10.

A special thank you goes to Hilary Cronheim, Special Collections Librarian at the USGA. Hilary was not only very helpful during my visit to the USGA Library, but responded to all of my subsequent requests for information in a prompt, professional, and cheerful manner.

Erin Shellaway, Saucon Valley Country Club Member Services, and George Mowers, Club Archivist, were both very helpful during my research of club archives.

Martin Emeno, Golf Association of Philadelphia Director of Operations, proved once again to be the epitome of professionalism and efficiency. Tony Regina, GAP's Assistant Director of Communications, did a marvelous job editing the compilation of home movies included in the companion video.

Mark Wogenrich of *The Morning Call* and Karl Gilbert were both available for help and advice whenever needed.

Sincere thanks to all those interviewed: Clyde Oskin Jr, Jim White, Tom McHale, Bill McGuiness, Wade Borg, John Benson, Jim Roney, Jerry Hoesteter, Michael Cumberpatch, Rick McCall, and Debbie Moore.

In his role as a member of the Lehigh Valley Golf Hall of Fame nominating committee, Brian McCall conducted detailed research into the life of Eugene Grace. Brian has always been very helpful and eager to share his research information with me.

I wish to express my sincere thanks to Arnold Palmer and Doc Giffin. It goes without saying, when the most famous figure in golf responds to a request for information within two business days---that's impressive! This speaks volumes about Mr. Palmer and what he stands for.

Nancy Meyer, a longtime family friend and published author, provided much appreciated editing and publishing advice.

Saucon Valley member Jim White not only shared his personal experiences from the 1951 U.S. Amateur, but is responsible for creating the five volume photographic record of the 1951 U.S. Amateur that resides in club archives. Jim dedicated these volumes to his late father, Daniel White, longtime Club Manager at Saucon Valley. The wide variety of information contained in these volumes proved invaluable. Jim also spent several hours helping me identify the people and places appearing in the video record of the 1951 U.S. Amateur.

Long time Saucon Valley member Debbie Moore, grandniece of Eugene Grace, also helped identify those appearing in the 1951 video record.

Another Saucon Valley member, Tom McHale, shared his personal experiences from the 1951 U.S. Amateur. Tom also provided me with a copy of the 1951 U.S. Amateur Championship program from his personal collection. Most importantly, Tom shared his childhood memories of hero and friend, Jim McHale. Tom's recollections encouraged me to contact Marty Emeno of the Golf Association of Philadelphia and Hilary Cronheim at the USGA Library for additional information on Jim McHale. The result of this research brought to light the remarkable life, and playing career, of arguably the greatest player in Saucon Valley Country Club history.

For me, next to meeting Billy Maxwell, the most rewarding aspect of this entire project is the knowledge that research conducted for this book directly contributed to the induction of Jim McHale into the Golf Association of Philadelphia Hall of Fame. James B. McHale Jr. (1916-1997) is the sole member of GAP's Hall of Fame class of 2015. Just as it was with Eugene Grace's chance introduction to the game of golf during a vacation to Pinehurst in 1909, one never knows what lies around life's next turn, or where it might lead.

A debt of gratitude is owed to all committee members and volunteers of the 1951 U.S. Amateur Championship. Most of these folks are no longer with us, but their contributions live on in club archives. The statistical information available on the tournament and the level of detail contained in committee reports is nothing short of amazing. Passion and commitment to excellence is evident in everything they did and stands as a great example for all of us to follow.

Last, but certainly not least, sincere appreciation goes to my wife, Carolyn, the real author in the family. In addition to serving as editor Carolyn provided constant encouragement and advice throughout the entire process. This project reached a successful conclusion primarily due to her help and support.

CHAPTER ONE

Abilene

"Genuine beginnings begin within us, even when they are brought to our attention by external opportunities."

William Throsby Bridges

Billy Maxwell grew up on a golf course in the small West Texas town of Abilene. His father leased the Willow Springs Golf Course and directed the operation as both the head professional, and greenskeeper. Born in 1929, Billy and twin brother Bob were the youngest of William Ownby (W.O.) and Eula Ann Maxwell's seven children. The Maxwell family, three boys and four girls lived in a modest home located just off the 4th fairway of the Abilene Country Club, and within 100 yards of neighboring Willow Springs. In the midst of The Great Depression every member of the family was expected to pitch in. Both Billy and Bob went to work on the golf course at an early age. As Billy fondly remembers, "We would mow the greens, and do all the little chores around the golf course...we grew up in a little country town playing golf, it was great." Older brother, W.O. Jr., spent many of those years serving in the U. S. Navy, but eventually returned home to help out as well.

The Maxwell twins grew up admiring the accomplishments of legendary golfer Bobby Jones, but never actually watched Jones play the game. During those times, especially in a small Texas town, there wasn't much information available about golf. With no visual awareness of the mechanics of the golf swing, Billy and Bob learned the game the old fashioned way – in the dirt! "We just went out and did it," Billy explained, "We picked it up by playing. If we had a question about how to grip it properly, and such, we'd just ask our dad or someone. We didn't know much about practice. We just played. As a youngster you'd play with a member or friend of a member."

The unpredictable West Texas weather and the hard Abilene soil proved to be an excellent teacher. Rather than focus on swinging the club in a perfect manner, the boys learned how to hit a variety of shots under diverse conditions. "I tell everybody if the south wind isn't blowing, just watch the sky, because if it isn't blowing, something is brewing," Billy explained.

Regarding any specific method he employed, Billy offered, "I just tried to hit in the middle of the clubface, and try to hit that same spot every time." Billy developed a strong work ethic early on, and was heavily influenced by the good example of Abilene Country Club's assistant pro Cleutus Duty. Cleutus constantly impressed upon young Billy the importance of total commitment in all aspects of the game.

Brother Bob was a natural left-hander but played golf right-handed. "Early on dad broke all of Bob's left-handed clubs, and insisted he learn to play right-handed," Billy said. Billy is also quick to point out fellow Texans Byron Nelson and Ben Hogan were both natural left-handers, but learned to play the game from the right side. Unsure if conventional wisdom determined it advantageous for a left handed person to play right handed, Billy offered, "I do know there wasn't good left-handed equipment available in those days."

Both brothers developed quickly, and through constant competition pushed each other to greater heights. One bit of Texas golf lore involving the Maxwell twins occurred in 1946 when, as 16 year-olds, the boys were pitted against each other in the finals of the Abilene City Championship. Both brothers shot 64, but Bob prevailed 1 up in the match play format. "Bob and I were very close, but during the match there was no talking. We let the clubs do the talking," Billy remembers. "It was just fun to play." Referring to Bob, Billy stated, "He beat me every time we played each other."

Over the years, perhaps influenced by the example of Byron Nelson, Bob became more interested in instruction rather than playing, and ended up devoting his career to teaching. He worked at the Colonial Country Club in Ft. Worth before moving to New York. Bob spent nearly ten years at the Century Country Club in Purchase, New York. While at Century he met a promising young player from The Creek Club by the name of Jerry Pittman. Pittman would go on to play in the Masters and win the Metropolitan Open twice. He would also become the longtime head professional at both Saucon Valley Country Club and Seminole Golf Club.

In addition to a very accomplished career in golf, Billy remembers Jerry Pittman leaving his opponents choking on his dust in another sport as well. "He was a real good card player...he'd play cards for real," Billy exclaimed.

Billy and Bob both played for Coach Fred Cobb on the golf team at North Texas State. Joining them on the team was a youngster from Plainview, Texas, named Don January. Beginning in 1950 they would lead North Texas to three consecutive NCAA Division I Golf Championships. The Screaming Eagles also won in 1949 making it four in a row for Coach Cobb and State. At North Texas Billy met his future wife, Mary Katherine (M. K.), while helping with a golf class. "There were so many students they had to split up the class, and Coach Cobb assigned me and other golf team members as instructors," Billy explained. Coincidentally, teammate Don January met his wife, Pat, in the same manner.

Long before his college days, Billy was also known as "The West Texas Cyclone." He was already building a reputation as a young player with tremendous potential. Billy won his first tournament, the Abilene Junior Championship, when he was 12. He successfully defended his crown the following three years, and in 1947 won another six amateur tournaments in West Texas.

Billy was featured in an article appearing in the May 5, 1948 issue of Golfworld. In part it reads:

> *"Sun-burned young Billy Maxwell, 17 year-old senior from St. Joseph's Academy, Abilene, proved in convincing fashion over the long Cedar Crest Golf Club layout in Dallas that he is the best teen-age golfer in Texas. The long distance slugger from the wind swept West Texas plains won the 8th annual Texas high school championship over the 6,700 yard municipal course by defeating another youngster from the plains country, husky Ross Mitchell of Lubbock, 9 and 8, in a 36 hole final of the prep classic."*

The tournament attracted 116 players from 31 schools across the state. With several West Texas titles under his belt Billy Maxwell was the king of Texas junior golf.

On August 11, 1948, Harry Gage of The Dallas News wrote:

> *"Brightest star on Texas links is stocky square-shouldered Billy Maxwell of Abilene. Nine years in the making, this bushy-browed West Texas youngster is looked upon by Lone Star golfanactics as the future Moses who will lead Texas from the wilderness after the Hogans, Demarets, and Mangrums have folded their tents and trudged out of the national golf scene."*

In The Dallas News article, Gage goes on to write, "In June of 1948, Maxwell fired the strokes that really told Texas golfers they had a find." Eighteen year old Billy competed in the Texas PGA Championship as an amateur, finishing runner-up to champion Byron Nelson. Nelson was forced to birdie the 72nd hole to defeat young Billy by just one stroke. Billy's score of 289 was 8 strokes clear of the next amateur.

This wasn't the first time Billy had gone head to head against Nelson. The two played each other in an exhibition match the previous year with Billy coming out on top shooting a remarkable 62. No wonder Lord Byron declared Billy a better player at age 18 than himself!

CHAPTER TWO

Legends of Texas Golf

"The only thing you should force in a golf swing is the club back in the bag."

Byron Nelson

Nelson, well known for mentoring younger players, took an interest in Billy, and the entire North Texas State team for that matter. "He was always good...would always say something nice," Billy explained. "When we all went to college up at North Texas, his ranch was only 15 miles from school, and he'd come down and play with the team every now and again. He was one-of-a-kind."

Billy recalls another legend of Texas golf – Ben Hogan. "I played with Ben Hogan a lot of times, both as an amateur and as a pro." He remembers the first time he played with Hogan. His good friend Ernie Vossler Jr. set it up. "Ernie's father was a member at Colonial, and he asked me, 'Do you want to play with Ben Hogan today?'" Billy continues, "You hear all these stories about him, but I really liked him. He was a very generous person, but he was the type of guy that didn't want to meet anyone. He just wanted to play golf. At Colonial he'd go down to the practice tee, and wouldn't come back until it was dark. If someone put down some balls to practice next to him he would just move."

One day at Colonial, Billy was introduced to Hogan's precision off the tee. "We were playing a par-4 dogleg right with a creek hugging the right side. Ben hit his drive, and I said to Ernie, Ummm, I don't know. I think that may be in the water. Ernie started laughing, and said 'How'd you like that drive, Ben?' 'I liked it,' Hogan replied. 'Billy says you're close to the water hazard over on the right there,'" Hogan remained stoic. Billy describes what happened next, "When we got up there that ball was right on the pipeline in the middle of the fairway!"

In his 1996 book _Hogan_ Curt Sampson explains both Hogan and Nelson grew up at the same golf course Glen Garden Country Club in Fort Worth, Texas. They both caddied at the club, and competed against each other in the annual caddie tournament during those years. "Byron Nelson, and Ben Hogan came from the same place, but they were different as night and day," Billy said. "I remember some other fellas that came from the same caddie yard were really good players also -- maybe not tour players, but very good amateurs...someone was teaching them well."

As it turns out, that "someone" was a young assistant pro from Oklahoma named Jack Grout. Grout started working at Glen Garden Country Club around the same time Hogan and Nelson caddied at the club. Jack Grout would later become the Head Professional at the Scioto Country Club in Columbus, Ohio. While at Scioto he would gain fame as the man who taught Jack Nicklaus how to play golf. Grout remained Nicklaus' only instructor for 25 years.

Another Texas golf legend, Jimmy Demaret, was one of Billy's favorite people. Billy said, "I really liked Jimmy Demaret. He was the greatest golf pro I ever met in my life...and fun...if you wanted someone to sing, or dance, or anything, he'd just play the part." Ben Hogan felt the same way about Demaret. "Hogan loved Jimmy Demaret. He loved that guy! He (Demaret) would needle Hogan, and get him laughing like crazy."

Jimmy Demaret's flamboyant personality was enhanced by his bright-colored clothing, which he had specially made. The three-time Masters champion's nickname was "The Wardrobe." Regarding Demaret's reputation as a fashion trendsetter, Billy responded, "Oh yeah. Everybody that was a pro had to get some of those slacks he wore."

When asked why so many great players came out of Texas, Billy responded, "I think they were more hungry than the others."

CHAPTER THREE

Spirit of the Game

"One secret of success in life is for a man to be ready for his opportunity when it comes."

Benjamin Disraeli

Francis Ouimet, a twenty year-old from Brookline, Massachusetts, delivered golf to the masses when he became the first amateur to win the U.S. Open in 1913. Ten years after Ouimet's victory the number of amateur players in the U.S. grew from 350,000 to over 2 million, and many new golf courses were built, including a large number of public venues.

Beginning with his 1923 U.S. Open victory at the Inwood Country Club in Long Island, New York, amateur Bobby Jones of Atlanta secured golf's place on the map in the United States. "Emperor" Jones won an incredible 9 major championships from 1923 to 1929 and topped it off in 1930 by winning all four major championships in the same year --- the U.S. Amateur, U.S. Open, British Amateur, and The Open Championship

(British Open). Legendary sportswriter O.B. Keeler, borrowing a bridge term, called it the "Grand Slam," and the name stuck. Later, in an attempt to describe the near impossibility of such a feat, George Trevor of the *New York Sun* coined the term "The Impregnable Quadrilateral." Bobby Jones remains the only individual athlete to be honored with more than one ticker-tape parade through New York City's Canyon of Heroes. Jones was honored in both 1926 and 1930 after his victories in the British Amateur, and Open Championships.

By 1951, professionals Ben Hogan, Byron Nelson, and Sam Snead had all made their mark, but amateur Jones was still revered and remained the most famous golfer in the world. Despite his retirement from competition twenty years earlier, Jones remained very influential and maintained a high golf profile primarily through product endorsements, instructional films, and his involvement with the Masters tournament, which he co-founded in 1934 with Clifford Roberts.

The era immediately following World War II was a very optimistic and almost magical time. With respect to golf – amateur golf was king. It was a time before huge purses and lucrative endorsement deals. As a result, the top players didn't turn professional immediately following success on the national scene as they might today. Many of the career amateurs appearing in the field at Saucon Valley enjoyed a type of celebrity status, much like the modern-day PGA Tour player.

The popularity of amateur golf was demonstrated in a September 9, 1951 article appearing in the Sports Section of *The New York Times*. Blaring across the headline was the announcement "Chapman Heads Metropolitan Golf Association Handicap Rating at Plus 1." The article went on to list all 3,498 individual members of the MGA and their respective handicaps.

It's hard to imagine, but in some instances amateur golf even garnered more attention than the NFL. For example, the same day the U.S. Amateur dominated headlines in the Allentown Morning Call, and thousands lined up at Saucon Valley to attend the championship, a small advertisement appeared at the bottom of the same page announcing an upcoming game between the Philadelphia Eagles and New York Giants. Urging fans with the statement "Don't Miss This One," the ad proclaimed "There's No Football Like Pro Football."

Contributing to the 51st Amateur Championship program, Bobby Jones wrote the following:

> *"In each decade, at least, of our golfing history we have had one or more amateur golfers capable of competing on equal terms with the best professionals. There have been many more, there will be many in the field at Saucon Valley...At this time when many sports are suspect, it is comforting to reflect upon the strict requirements of the USGA for the retention by a player of amateur status, and the fervor with which insistence upon fulfillment is made...In the truest sense, the championship at Saucon Valley will be a real Amateur Championship."*

In his essay entitled "*Saucon Valley and The Present Day Amateur Golfer,*" Francis Ouimet offers us a prophetic description of what he calls the new amateur:

> *"Today we have a new crop of amateur golfers who may be called the modern type. They hit the ball colossal distances and can play the other strokes as well. There are not just a handful but literally dozens of them. That is what you will see at Saucon when the tournament gets under way."*

Chick Evans summed up the relationship between Saucon Valley and its founder, Eugene Grace, quite nicely when he wrote:

> *"Mr. Grace is one of the best loved golfers of the country...Mr. Grace is a man who loves golf for its own sake. He loves the good shots of the game and he learned to make them. More than most men, however, he realized that the making of good shots must be encouraged by good courses. There were good courses around Bethlehem, but Mr. Grace's ideas went beyond anything that had yet been achieved, and his vision led to the building of Saucon Valley by his associates and himself. Many players in the USGA's 51st U.S. Amateur Championship will leave Bethlehem with the justifiable impression that Saucon Valley is the choicest course upon which the tournament has ever been played."*

In a welcome letter appearing in the championship program, Grace expressed his feelings on the importance of amateur golf, and amateurism in sports. Grace, in part, penned the following:

> *"If I were asked to name the controlling thought that is governing us in acting as hosts on the occasion, it would be to emphasize the importance of amateurism in sports...We welcome the opportunity of serving the interests of golf in this manner."*

Born August 27, 1876, in Cape May, New Jersey, Eugene Gifford Grace was the son of sea captain John Wesley Grace and Rebecca (Morris) Grace. Bright and athletic, Grace was very competitive and driven to excellence even at a young age. For Grace, anything worth doing was worth doing well. Whether in business or his personal life, he excelled at all he did. He graduated from Lehigh University in 1899 at the top of his class with a degree in Electrical Engineering, and was named class valedictorian. Despite a heavy academic load, he still found time to captain the Lehigh baseball team. Grace was the squad's starting shortstop with a batting average over .400. His ability was so highly regarded the Boston Braves offered him a contract. To the dismay of friends, he declined the higher salary offered by the Braves, and after graduation hung up the baseball gear to begin his "life's work" with the Bethlehem Steel Corporation.

Grace's first job at the company was electric crane operator making $1.80 a day. It wasn't long before his ambition and strong determination to succeed moved him up the corporate ladder. In 1902 he was named Superintendent of Yards and Transportation, and by 1908 he was General Manager. Chairman Charles Schwab discovered the young man's genius for organization and production, and as they say, the rest is history. In 1913, at the age of 37, Grace was named president of the company.

It was during a vacation to Pinehurst, North Carolina, in 1909, when Grace was first introduced to golf. Searching for some exercise, on a whim, he took a golf lesson. Very few details are known, except that the golf professional's name was "Mr. Green." What we do know -- Eugene Grace was absolutely smitten. After returning to Bethlehem, Grace approached his new hobby with his typical fervor, and within ten years won the club championship at the Country Club of Northampton County (Northampton Country Club).

Ever the perfectionist, Grace spent most of his spare time working to improve his game. Beginning in 1912 his game underwent a complete makeover. During this period he made it a point to play only with those he considered better than he was. As a result, Grace was able to transform himself into one of the finest amateurs in the Lehigh Valley.

During World War I, he would routinely play exhibition matches with golf icons Chick Evans, Harry Vardon, and Ted Ray to raise money for The War Relief Fund. It is believed Grace first met Bobby Jones, only 15 years old at the time, during an exhibition match benefitting the Red Cross. Playing with the greats of the game set the bar pretty high, and Grace was determined to elevate his game. Mr. Grace shot in the sixties many times, and even in later years his game remained very sharp. He shot his age at 67, but considered a 71 at Pine Valley, in his 71st year, his greatest accomplishment. It was during that round he beat host professional George Fazio by two strokes. For several years it is reported Fazio delighted in telling the story of his defeat at the hands of "Bethlehem's Mr. Golf."

Having mastered and defined his own golf game, Grace turned his attention in another direction. As Chick Evans had said of Grace, "There were very nice courses already in the area, but Grace's personal vision went far beyond anything that had previously been accomplished." Grace's determination would lead to the building of Saucon Valley.

In 1920, Grace, along with Bethlehem attorney Howard A. Lehman, C. A. Buck, and 16 other business leaders from Bethlehem, would acquire 208 acres of land along the Saucon Creek in Upper Saucon Township, Lehigh County. The name Saucon is derived from the Native American "SAKUNK," meaning "a small stream flowing into a big stream." Formerly a dairy farm, the property was purchased for $25,000 (approximately $300,000 today).

Although contractors were asked to donate the cement for the construction of the swimming pool, and the property's farmhouse would serve as the first clubhouse, there would be no cutting corners when it came to the golf course. The original plan called for a nine-hole course, but this was far too modest for Grace. Renowned golf organizer, and course designer, Herbert Strong of England, would be Grace's choice for architect. Strong was a professional golfer and fine player --- finishing 5th in the famous 1913 U.S. Open. He was also a founding member of the PGA of America in 1916 and later served as the association's first Secretary-Treasurer. Strong had just finished a restoration project at the Inwood Country Club on Long Island when Grace convinced him to come to Bethlehem. Strong's philosophy of "building natural beauty into every possible feature of play," convinced Grace that he was the right man for the job. Later, Grace would hire Strong's younger brother, Leonard, to be course superintendent.

During the autumn of 1920 while Strong walked off the course through the valley's meadowlands and grain fields, it was not uncommon to see as many as 100 members working to dismantle old farm buildings on the property. Good old fashioned "stone picking" contests were also a popular pastime.

Grace would play a significant role in the design of the course as well. Having played all the great courses, both here and abroad, Grace felt compelled to influence the design of certain holes on the course by leaving his personal mark. Following the example of famed architects Seth Raynor and Charles Blair McDonald, he insisted certain famous design features be included at Saucon Valley. This included a Biarritz style green on the par-4 12th (originally a par-3). This particular design was adapted from Willie Dunn's original "chasm" hole in Biarritz, France, and featured a deep trough running across the green. The island green on the par-3 11th was another of Grace's ideas. It should be noted, in fashioning replica holes, the particular geography of the course was taken into consideration giving these designs similar, yet distinct characteristics. For example, on the 11th hole, instead of surrounding the green with water, the same effect was achieved using deep bunkers.

Later in the 1940's, Grace would retain Perry Maxwell and William Gordon to continue improving the course until it reached a pinnacle of perfection. This high level of excellence led the USGA to choose Saucon Valley for the site of the 1951 U.S. Amateur over Five Farms Country Club in Baltimore. The USGA was completely satisfied with the course. The only suggestion made was to narrow a few fairways. The course was praised by many of the contestants in 1951 as "the finest on which the USGA Amateur has ever been played."

Eugene Grace served as President of Bethlehem Steel from 1913 to 1945 and Chairman of the Board from 1945 to 1957. Although he never held an official office at Saucon Valley Country Club, he assumed the role of "Patriarch" and remained the driving force behind the growth and success of the club until his death in 1960.

CHAPTER FOUR

The Big Dance

"Golf is the closest game to the game we call life. You get bad breaks from good shots; you get good breaks from bad shots – but you have to play the ball where it lies."

Bobby Jones

When Billy Maxwell and his fellow competitors arrived at Saucon Valley, they were completely astounded. "None of us had ever seen a golf course in that kind of condition. The whole thing was so perfectly manicured," Billy said.

In anticipation of hosting the U.S. Amateur, Grace had all the grass on the course killed and replaced with new bent grass in 1949. In a May 2015 interview, Clyde Oskin Jr., reigning Saucon Valley Club Champion from 1948 to 1952, confirms all the grass being dead for a period of time, but said the membership didn't know why.

It's unlikely anyone asked Mr. Grace for an explanation.

A story appearing in the September 9, 1951 issue of *The New York Times* reported Mr. Grace employed a maintenance crew six days a week for two years for the sole purpose of "reseeding the course, and replacing divots." Saucon Valley member Debbie Moore, grand-niece of Eugene Grace, recalls seeing the crew form a line four men across moving up each fairway with military precision picking weeds and filling divots as they went.

"Never have I played a better course," stated Walker Cup Captain Willie Turnesa. "Not a single flaw from tee to green," declared British Amateur Champion Dick Chapman. Chick Evans shared the following, "Saucon Valley is hard to write about because there's not just one outstanding feature to lead off with—everything's outstanding."

Members of the press were equally generous with their praise. Bob Drum, of *The Pittsburgh Press* reported, "...it is fitting that Saucon Valley be called a golfing Utopia. Both from a player's and writer's standpoint."

"This place was so plush... we even joked about it," recalled John Owens in a 1987 interview with John Kunda of *The Morning Call*. Owens was one of six players who played in the 1951 Amateur at Saucon Valley, and returned for the U.S. Senior Amateur in 1987. The other players who came back 36 years later included Bill Hyndman, Ed Tutwiler, Harold Kirkpatrick, and Keith Campbell. Billy Jo Patton returned in 1987, but as a member of the USGA Senior Amateur Committee.

Mr. Grace's striving for perfection went beyond the condition of the golf course. The previous year the clubhouse underwent an entire modernization and expansion. "The hospitality was also off the charts," said longtime Saucon Valley member Jim White, who as a youngster caddied in the championship for Tommy Barnes of Atlanta. After Barnes lost in the third round, White was reassigned to the media tent. He spent the remainder of the week as a "runner" delivering telegrams throughout club property. Between assignments he managed to watch portions of several matches. White remembers witnessing a particularly interesting maintenance technique employed during championship week. "After a player hit a shot from the fairway, a man wearing a little hat, and carrying a small bucket of dirt would appear from the woods to fill the divot. He then disappeared just as quickly," White explained.

In the September 21, 1951 issue of Golfweek, Bob Harlow wrote:

> *"Just as Mr. Grace's guiding hand appears in the course, so did it in the production of the 1951 amateur championship...they knew that the amateur championship was Mr. Grace's show and they gave their best to make it tops. Operation Saucon Valley was in the hands of executives no golf tournament could possibly afford to hire. They did the job."*

"I didn't know Mr. Grace personally. I met him a time or two, but he did a world of good for golf," Billy shared.

Beginning with practice round week there were 114 members of the working press assigned to cover the championship. Of this number, there were 73 newspaper correspondents, 12 radio announcers, 21 photographers, and 8 magazine representatives. Everyone raved about the state of the art media center, which was located between the 9th and 18th holes. One reporter referred to the accommodations as "the most palatial press headquarters in golfing history."

In addition to the star-studded field there were also legendary members of the press in attendance. Lincoln Werden was assigned to cover the championship as a correspondent for The New York Times. Werden was Lou Gehrig's classmate in both high school and at Columbia University. Today, the Metropolitan Golf Writers Association annual award for "Outstanding Journalism" is named *The Lincoln Werden Award.*

Oscar Fraley worked the championship as a sports writer for UPI. His by-line appeared several times that week in the Bethlehem Globe-Times. In his spare time Fraley liked to write crime stories. In 1956, while covering another sporting event, he had a chance meeting with Eliot Ness. They became friends and later agreed to collaborate on Ness's memoirs. The result was the best seller *The Untouchables*, and much fame and fortune for both Ness and Fraley. Later in the 1960's, Fraley would become lead consultant to the successful television series by the same name.

Fraley didn't need to cover any golf tournaments after that.

With regard to the media center --- attention was paid to the smallest detail. The following statement appeared in the *Report of the Program and Publicity Committee* filed after the championship:

> *"The individual tables for the newsmen and the Western Union operators were specially constructed for the Press Tent. These were designed 26 inches high for the convenience of typewriter operation. These units, plus the fluorescent lighting delivering 32-foot candles of light in the Press Tent, were well worth the investment based on the comments received from all persons using this facility."*

Grace's meticulous preparation for the championship, and his desire for the course to present a challenge for the country's best players, justified making adjustments right up to last minute. Clyde Oskin remembers some of the work being done on the course. "He built a new tee on the 15th hole just prior to the tournament," Oskin said. After observing play during practice rounds, Grace was apparently dissatisfied with the length of the dogleg left, par-5. He ordered the installation of a new tee extending the hole's length to a prodigious 612 yards. At the time, this made Saucon Valley's 15th hole the longest hole in U.S. Amateur history.

In her book *Lifelong Looper, The Story of a Caddy Legend*, Cindy O'Krepki describes how a practice round double-eagle 2 on the par-5 first hole by Ken Venturi convinced Grace to move the green farther back and to the right. Saucon Valley legend Ross "Cotton" Young, the subject of O'Krepki's book, caddied for Dale Morey in the U.S. Amateur. Regarding the status of the first hole, Young stated, "Grace demanded the yardage be increased from 512 to 558 yards." Changes to the first green were completed immediately following the championship.

It was well-known Grace believed all par fives should be three-shot holes, and never reachable in two strokes. It has even been reported Grace argued with Bobby Jones and Clifford Roberts over the length of the par fives on the back nine of the Augusta National Golf Club. The discussion became so emotional that Grace, a founding member of Augusta National, threatened to leave the club unless the 13th and 15th holes were lengthened. In the end, no changes were made, resulting in "E.G." spending his remaining years vacationing with other giants of industry at the prestigious Palmetto Golf Club in nearby Aiken, South Carolina.

Ken Venturi was also part of another very famous story involving the U.S. Amateur at Saucon Valley. During a practice round as Venturi and Harvie Ward waited to tee off on the short dogleg right, par-4, 13th, they were approached by Mr. Grace, who had been watching play from the nearby West Terrace. Inquiring about their general impression of the course, Mr. Grace also asked for their opinion of the 13th hole.

"It's not much of a hole really. You can drive it up the left side all the way to the green," was the response.

No definitive source exists to confirm who responded. The most common held belief gives credit to Venturi, but one thing is for certain, the comments set in motion a very interesting chain of events. When the first group arrived at the thirteenth tee the following morning, they were greeted by four newly installed bunkers lined up along the left side of the fairway.

"There were no bunkers on the left of #13, and then all of a sudden they were there," recalls Clyde Oskin.

Jim White remembers the situation well, and confirms the overnight installation of the fairway bunkers in a 2015 interview. "That's exactly how it happened," White stated. "I'm not sure who it was that spoke up, but that is exactly what was said."

Over the years Green Committee members often mused over the shape of the fairway bunkers on #13 of the Old Course (today Saucon Valley features three championship courses – Grace, Weyhill, and the original Old Course). The shape of these four bunkers didn't match the other bunkers on the hole and displayed distinct Gordon characteristics. The photographic evidence in club archives showing William Gordon on the property with Mr. Grace during championship week, combined with these eye witness accounts, confirms one of the more interesting legends of Saucon Valley and Eugene Grace.

Mr. Grace's commitment to maintaining a spirit of pure amateurism went beyond the actual competition. The Championship Program featured over 70 pages of beautiful content, but did not contain a single advertisement. Another example involved a club vendor. In order to accommodate the thirst requirements of the large crowds expected to attend the championship, a local Coca-Cola distributor was contracted to provide mobile refreshment stands. When the trailers arrived at the club, each one sported a bright red Coca-Cola sign on the side. Before the tournament began Grace had all the brand names covered with white paint. Grace's decision didn't seem to interfere with sales, as the vendor enjoyed a robust business. Warmer than normal temperatures contributed to an incredible amount of the soft drink consumed during the event. Member Tom McHale, a sixth grader at the time, remembers that several weeks after the conclusion of the tournament, maintenance crews and members were still picking up empty Coke bottles which had been strewn all over the club property.

With the many thousands of spectators attending the tournament, it's hard to imagine how many empty bottles were discarded. Fifty-five years later fragments were still showing up. During the Old Course restoration in 2006, several hundred broken Coke bottles were unearthed during excavation of the new tee on the par-5 15th hole.

CHAPTER FIVE

Love at First Sight

"It's a funny thing, the more I practice the luckier I get"

Arnold Palmer

The 51st Amateur Championship of the USGA set a new record for total entrants. The 1,426 entries exceeded the previous mark of 1,220 set in 1948 at the Memphis Country Club. The eligible field for the Championship consisted of 200 players. Sectional Qualifying rounds would determine 189 contestants, with 11 players exempt from qualifying based on previous championship victories. The following players were exempt from qualifying:

Sam Urzetta................................1950 U.S. Amateur
Charles R. Coe...........................1949 U.S. Amateur
William P. Turnesa ....1938, 1948 U.S. Amateur; 1947 British Am

Stanley E. Bishop........................1946 U.S. Amateur
Richard D. Chapman..................1940 U.S. Amateur; 1951 British Am
Charles Evans, Jr........................1916, 1920 U.S. Amateur
Frank R. Stranahan.....................1948, 1950 British Amateur
Robert Sweeny...........................1937 British Amateur
William C. Mawhinney.................1950 Canadian Amateur
David Stanley..............................1951 USGA Amateur Public Links
Keith Tommy Jacobs, Jr..............1951 USGA Junior Amateur

Robert Sweeny, 1937 British Amateur champion and R.A.F. war hero, was the only exempt player not to play in the championship. USGA entry guidelines are strict, and Sweeny's entry did not arrive by the deadline.

In an August 22, 1951 news release the USGA explained the qualifying process:

> *"Never before in the history of the USGA was it so difficult for a golfer to get into the Open Championship proper as it was this year, and this same situation now holds true for the 51st Amateur Championship, which will be played September 10-15 at the Saucon Valley Country Club, Bethlehem, Pa. There was an all-time record entry of 1,426. Of these, 1,415 will compete for 189 places in sectional qualifying rounds; thus, an average of one out of every 7.5 competitors will qualify for the Championship proper."*

> *"The 36-hole qualifying rounds will take place Thursday, August 28th, at 32 points scattered throughout the nation. A total of 36 qualifying tests were originally scheduled, but rounds were cancelled because of insufficient entries at Honolulu; Des Moines, Iowa; Albuquerque, N.M.; and Salt Lake City, Utah."*
>
> *"The 189 sectional qualifiers will be joined in the Championship proper by 11 exempt players to make a total field of 200. This is 10 less than in 1950, when 210 took part in the match play."*
>
> *"....The allotment of qualifier's places in each section was determined by the size and the strength of the playing field."*

There were 12 players competing at Midland, Texas, with 2 qualifying spots up for grabs. Richard Jennings of Lubbock led the field with rounds of 71-66=137. Billy Maxwell fired 70-68=138 to finish second, and earn the final spot.

The largest qualifying field was in New York, where 177 players competed for 21 spots. The size of the field made it necessary to use two golf courses, The Meadow Brook Club and Wheatley Hills Golf Club. Frank Strafaci won the medal in New York with a score of 73-73=146. "The Golfing Judge," Joe Gagliardi, squeezed in with 77-73=150.

New Orleans and Minneapolis shared honors for the smallest field at eight, with one qualifier advancing from each. Richard Collard matched Strafaci's numbers exactly (73-73=146) to move on from New Orleans, while Ade Simonsen blistered the field at Woodhill Country Club in the Minneapolis qualifier with a score of 66-70=136.

The qualifier held in Lincoln, Nebraska, displayed a local flavor. Fourteen of the seventeen contestants were members of the host club, Country Club of Lincoln. So much for home course advantage---the two qualifiers who advanced were from out of town.

Major Robert E. Lee found no victory north of the Mason-Dixon Line, failing to qualify in Cincinnati. Lakeside Golf Club's Forrest Tucker, fresh off his film role as Pfc. Al Thomas in *The Sands of Iwo Jima* gave it his best Hollywood try, but failed to make the grade in Los Angeles. Despite having a regulation putting green installed on his lawn so he could practice his short game during his busy filming schedule, big screen mega-star Randolph Scott failed to advance past the local qualifier in L.A. as well.

Success was in store for Brigadier General Ken Rogers in the Tulsa, Oklahoma qualifier. Due to his premature gray coiffure the WW II general was nicknamed "The Silver Fox." Rogers proved very wily at Saucon Valley, making it all the way to the third round of match play before bowing to Mid-Atlantic golf legend Ed Johnston on the 19th hole.

In Denver, three members of the same family made it. William Carey Jr. tied for medalist honors with a score of 74-70=144. When the remaining two qualifiers were unable to make the trip, the first two alternates, Emerson Carey Jr., and Emerson Carey III answered the call. Even though each Carey lost in the first round; father, son, and nephew enjoyed an incredible week together at Saucon Valley. There have been several instances in U.S. Amateur history of a father and son competing in the same championship -- Saucon Valley member David Derminio and son Michael accomplished the feat in 2001 at the East Lake Golf Club in Atlanta. While it is nearly impossible to determine if any other instance exists of three family members competing in the same U.S. Amateur, it is certain "The Three Golfing Careys" share an extremely rare distinction.

The country's second largest qualifying field was in Philadelphia, with 153 hopefuls playing for 17 spots at The Philadelphia Cricket Club and Whitemarsh Valley Country Club. Howard Everitt of the Atlantic City Country Club shot 70-67=137 to capture medalist honors. Saucon Valley members who played, but failed to qualify, included 14-time club champion Clyde Oskin Jr., 7-time champion Ralph Hunsicker, Harold Bilheimer, Harvey Miller, and J. Wood Platt.

In later years Howard Everitt would provide the USGA with an autobiographical summary of his experience at the 1951 U.S. Amateur at Saucon Valley. In it he explains the circumstances surrounding his first round loss to Billy Key of Columbus, Georgia. Everitt writes:

> *"The course was ideal for my game, it was thoroughly enjoyable to play...Felt pretty good about the event winning the qualifying medal at Whitemarsh, and Philadelphia Cricket Club...At the time I was selling whiskey for the Publicker Co. of Phila. We did quite a nice business with Old Hickory brand whiskey in Allentown and I developed a friendship with Mike Dulik. His wife was away during the tournament and I was invited to stay at his home. He also, unbeknown to me, invited Bud Weiser (no pun intended), a sports writer for the Allentown paper, and Oscar Fraley to stay at his home. No excuses, but they got to playing cards and putting away some brew, a lot of it, and just stayed noisy all night. No one slept this night before the tournament. I recall going along very well, but faded badly losing No 16 and 18 too late to a fine player, Billy Key, 1 down."*

The outcome was very unfortunate for Everitt, one of Philadelphia's most decorated amateurs of all time. His record included playing in eight U.S. Amateurs, winning the Philadelphia Amateur, Patterson Cup, and Silver Cross titles, each three times, and the Pennsylvania Amateur Championship twice. In 2012 Howard Everitt was inducted into the Golf Association of Philadelphia Hall of Fame. Perhaps his most unheralded accomplishment in golf had nothing to do with his playing ability, but rather his friendship with a young up-and-coming golfer from Western Pennsylvania.

In 1954 Everitt was working publicity for Fred Waring at Shawnee-on-the-Delaware, and invited good friend Arnold Palmer to play in a tournament Mr. Waring called "The Young Masters." Waring had kidded Everitt after Palmer won the U.S. Amateur that year, he probably wouldn't come to his tournament. Everitt responded by saying, "not only would he come, but he was bringing his boss, and his boss' wife." At the time Palmer worked as a paint salesman. When Palmer arrived at Shawnee, Fred Waring's daughter, Dixie, and her friend Winnie Walzer, were in charge of entertainment.

A young woman caught Palmer's eye, and he finally blurted out "Who is that?" referring to Winnie. It was Howard Everitt who made the formal introduction. "When Arnie met Winnie it was love at first sight," said Everitt. After the tournament Palmer left to play in the Miami Open, but immediately returned to Shawnee to see Winnie. "I got this from the Deacon (Palmer's father) himself," said Everitt, "'Palmer said, Dad, I will never feel right until I go back to Shawnee and see whether I want to marry that girl.'" "I was there when Arnie came back," recalled Everitt. Winnie walked along while Palmer, Stan Dudas, and Ronnie Ward played eighteen holes. After the round Arnie proposed, and they were married shortly thereafter.

CHAPTER SIX

Guess Who's Coming to Dinner

"Comedy is simply a funny way of being serious"

Peter Ustinov

In his correspondence, Howard Everitt goes on to describe a special player's dinner hosted by the USGA and Saucon Valley Country Club. A veteran of many U. S. Amateur championships, Everitt writes, "I mention it because I believe it was the first and established a precedent which has been continued." Open to all contestants and their guests, the event was underwritten by the Bethlehem Steel Corporation, and took place at company headquarters in Bethlehem.

At first glance, an article in the September 21, 1951 issue of *Golf World* magazine appears to contradict Everitt's claim, by referring to the dinner as a "second annual affair." However, closer examination of the previous year's event reveals the gathering at Minneapolis Golf Club in 1950 was primarily a 50th anniversary celebration. The 1951 U. S. Amateur at Saucon

Valley is where the player's dinner stood on its own and the annual tradition began.

The following formal invitation went out to all the contestants at Saucon Valley. Of particular interest is the explanation for the purpose of the dinner:

TO QUALIFIERS FOR THE 1951 AMATEUR CHAMPIONSHIP

GENTLEMEN:

The Association cordially invites you to dinner Saturday, September 8 at 7:15 P.M. at the Main Dining Room of the Bethlehem Steel Company's General Office, Bethlehem, Pa. Dress will be informal.

The Saucon Valley Country Club cordially invites you to cocktails at 6:30 P.M. the same evening at the same place.

We should appreciate receiving your reply not later than Tuesday, September 4, via the attached form.

The Amateur Championship is the great get-together of our country's representative amateur golfers. Down through the years, ever since its start in 1895, the Championship has been not only a great competition and a constructive influence but a sort of fraternity meeting. Many fast friendships have been formed during Championship week.

Now the Championship's very size makes it difficult for all of us to see one another and to get to know one another as well as we should like. We thought it

would be pleasant for us to have at least one evening together; hence this invitation.

Perhaps you have some questions about golf and USGA affairs—about Rules, or amateur status, or implements and the ball. If so, jot them down on the attached form, and during the dinner evening we'll try to have them answered by the chairman of the appropriate USGA committee. We won't be able to handle all questions asked, but we'll do the best we can. The USGA is your USGA; you're entitled to know all you want to know about it. The USGA can hardly be more effective than you make it.

There'll be no long speeches---the evening will be devoted mainly to a friendly get-together and to your questions and our attempts at answers.

Sincerely,

JOHN D. AMES
Chairman, Championship Committee

As a result of his "elder" status, Chick Evans was invited by USGA Executive Secretary, Joe Dey, to speak at the dinner. Evans responded with a hand written note dated August 30, 1951:

> *"Of course, I would be pleased to try to do so if I am in Bethlehem on that day. As I have written the Committee, I may not arrive until September 9th in the afternoon because of the Waite Memorial Tournament at Shawnee. More than that Ester has invited her*

> *brother Roy Underwood, and his wife to join us at Shawnee that weekend...and also I am shy."*

Chick Evans was unable to make the dinner and was replaced at the last minute by the defending champion, Sam Urzetta. As it turned out, Urzetta proved to be a very worthy choice. Urzetta, 25, who served with the 2nd Infantry Division during World War II, gave a most compelling speech on what winning the U.S. Amateur meant to him and his family. An exceptionally articulate young man, he began his speech with an almost prayerful tone. Urzetta explained, "Our family lost a brother in the war and my mother never seemed to recover from this loss until I won the championship. After that my mother changed. I thank God that I was born in this great country where everybody has a chance to go out and play golf and win a championship."

It was said Sam Urzetta could have made a living on stage. He was able to transition from his somber message to a more light-hearted approach as he went on to say, "Winning the U.S. Amateur has made a great change in my life. I now have a job." He then began a comedic routine keeping the entire audience "in stitches" with a clever impersonation of R. Fleetwood Hiskuth, Honorable Mayor of Southport, England. He performed an interpretation of the The Lord Mayor congratulating the American Walker Cup team for their victory at Royal Birkdale earlier that summer. The "Honorable Mayor" extended his welcome to the "competing teams, to the officials, to the representatives of the international press, and to the thousands of victors which this historic match will attract," said Dale Morey. Morey continues, "Sam clearly articulated with distinguished English overtones and manner of speaking with which Mayor Hiskuth extended his greeting."

Morey remembers, "All Sam needed to give his rendition regal dynamics was an aristocratic English monocle," and went on to say, "No one on Broadway could have topped Sam that evening."

Urzetta's performance was remembered by contestants for many years to come, and to this day it is customary for the defending champion to speak at the annual player's dinner.

CHAPTER SEVEN

Who's Who

"If a man says he will shoot a hole in that post and make it bleed – don't bet him."

Chuck McCool

The list of participants in the 1951 U.S. Amateur reads like a Who's Who of golf. Although well-known in Texas golf circles, Billy Maxwell had not yet reached the same level of respect on the national scene. At 5' 7" and 157 pounds, the young red-head presented a less than imposing figure, and those unfamiliar with Billy's game looked upon him with a sense of disbelief. "Maxwell scarcely pivots, and plays his shots virtually flat footed," said Lincoln Werden of The New York Times. Werden went on to describe Billy as "a stocky athlete a little shorter than his caddie."

By his own admission Billy came into the tournament without any expectations. "My iron game was probably my best strength," he said. Saucon Valley would indeed demand a strong iron game, but a review of the talent-laden field would quickly reveal why no one picked the young college golfer from Texas to do much in the national championship.

The field for the 1951 U.S. Amateur featured the best players in the country. The top amateurs referred to by Bobby Jones and Francis Ouimet were all there. Joining defending champion Sam Urzetta of Rochester, New York, was 1950 runner-up and two-time British Amateur champ Frank Stranahan of Toledo, Ohio. Harvie Ward, widely considered the best amateur in the country, and his close friend Ken Venturi, fresh off his record setting victory in the Northern California Amateur, were both playing. Reigning British Amateur champion Dick Chapman, 1949 U.S. Amateur champ Charlie Coe, two time U.S. Amateur champion Willie Turnesa, 1951 Carolinas Open champion Billy Joe Patton, and Chet Sanok, recent winner over many top professionals in the New Jersey Open were also there, as well as 7-time Metropolitan Amateur champion Frank Strafaci and 1951 Indiana Amateur and Open champion Dale Morey.

The youngest player in the field was 16 year-old Keith Tommy Jacobs Jr., the 1951 U.S. Junior champion from Montebello, California. The pundits didn't take young Tommy very seriously. Joe Whritenour, writing in the Bethlehem Globe-Times, summed up Tommy's chances by saying, "He will probably win a match or two." Of course, Tommy Jacobs had other ideas.

Young players like Jacobs, fellow teenager Billy Picard, and Tommy's good friend David Stanley, 20, provided an interesting diversity to the otherwise veteran field. Several of the country's top young amateurs were missing from the field at Saucon Valley. Despite coming out on top of 15,000 juniors in the National Jaycee Amateur earlier that summer, Doug Sanders was unable to advance past local qualifying. Others were unavailable to play that year due to their military service. That list included Al Mengert, Mac Hunter, Gene Littler, and a young Coast Guard Recruit named Arnold Palmer.

One Saucon Valley Country Club member made the field. Jim McHale was a non-resident member from Philadelphia who also played club golf at Whitemarsh Valley Country Club and the Overbrook Golf Club.

James B. McHale Jr. was born in 1916 in Stockton, California. His father, James Bernard (J.B.) McHale, formerly of Miners Mills, Pennsylvania, played professional baseball briefly for the Boston Red Sox. Young Jim began playing golf left-handed, but switched to right-handed after learning he hit the ball better from the right side. In 1936, Craig Wood would hire McHale to be his assistant after McHale defeated Wood by ten strokes in the Riverside (California) Open earlier that year. In the late 1930's he moved to Philadelphia and went to work for pro Ed Dudley at the Philadelphia Country Club. During his time at Philadelphia Country Club, McHale would meet his future wife, Mary McCloskey. Mary's father, Matthew H. McCloskey, was a leader in Philadelphia politics and former United States Ambassador to Ireland.

McHale entered active military service in the summer of 1941. After serving as a Staff Sergeant with the 17th and 101st Airborne in Europe during World War II, he returned home and regained his amateur status. He excelled both nationally and internationally. McHale played in six U.S. Opens, 12 U.S. Amateurs, nine British Amateurs, and was a member of victorious Walker Cup teams in 1949 and 1951. He also competed in the 1950 Masters. At the St. Louis Country Club in 1947, his third round 65, and 30 on the front nine, both set new U.S. Open scoring records. The 65 scoring record stood for three years, while his 30 for nine holes would stand alone, until Arnold Palmer tied it in 1960 at Cherry Hills. It was not surpassed until Neal Lancaster shot 29 at Shinnecock Hills in 1995. In the 1950 U.S. Open at Merion he finished as Low Amateur and in 38th place overall. McHale won the Patterson Cup in 1948 and that same year also won the Philadelphia Open to become the first amateur to do so in 45 years. It would be another 23 years before amateur Bill Hyndman would accomplish the same feat.

In the early 1950's, when his busy tournament schedule would permit, Jim McHale routinely played weekend golf at Saucon Valley with wife Mary, an avid golfer herself, and their good friend, television personality Mike Douglas.

In addition to all the country's top players the field included several very famous names. Charles "Chick" Evans, 61, of Chicago, the 1916 U.S. Open and U.S. Amateur champion, was the oldest player in the field. Mr. Evans was playing in his 42nd consecutive U.S. Amateur Championship. He would eventually set the record of 50 consecutive appearances. Located in USGA archives is a hand written note from Chick Evans to Joe Dey. Evans wrote, "It is a tribute to a great game and to a great association that allows participation in its national championship that length of time."

One interesting bit of trivia involving Chick Evans had to do with the number of clubs he carried in competition. Beginning in 1938 the rules of golf limited the number of clubs carried by a player to fourteen. Prior to this rule change the number of clubs a player could carry was unlimited. Bobby Jones was known to play with as many as 20 clubs in his bag. Chick Evans, on the other hand, never carried more than seven clubs. When queried about his preference for so few clubs, Evans simply stated, "I only need seven."

Ironically, despite carrying only seven "clubs," Evans employed as many as four different putters at the same time. In his book <u>A Game of Golf: A Book of Reminiscence</u>, Francis Ouimet describes Evan's putting woes, "There was never a greater golfer than Evans when it came to driving and iron-club play, but all that good work was frequently wasted because of wretched putting."

Future USGA Presidents' Harton Semple and William Campbell played in the Amateur at Saucon Valley, as well as the future USGA Director of Rules and Competitions, P.J. Boatwright. As an aside, Harton Semple's daughter followed in her father's golf footsteps. Carol Semple Thompson is the winner of 10 national championships, including the 1973 U.S. Women's Amateur and is also a member of the World Golf Hall of Fame.

The brother of future USGA president William Battle, John S. Battle Jr., of Charlottesville, Virginia, also played. The son of the sitting Governor of Virginia, young Battle lost in the first round 6 and 5 to Billy Maxwell's cross-town rival, Ed Hopkins, of Abilene, Texas.

As previously mentioned, Edward Johnston of Towson, Maryland, played at Saucon Valley, and made it all the way to the fourth round before bowing to Robert Eckis Jr. of New York. Johnston is credited with founding the long-standing Mason-Dixon Matches in 1951. The matches feature teams representing the Golf Association of Philadelphia and the Mid-Atlantic Golf Association, and remain a very popular competition to this day.

H. H. Haverstick Jr. of Pennsylvania's Lancaster Country Club played in the championship. Three years earlier Haverstick captured the 1948 Pennsylvania Amateur Championship on his home course. On the way to the title he defeated a 19 year-old Arnold Palmer in the second round by a score of 3 and 2.

Haverstick's second round match at Saucon Valley versus Dr. George Trainor of the Monroe Golf Club in New York "started off with a bang." On the 516 yard, par-5 first hole, the long hitting Trainor powered a three iron onto the green in two. With Haverstick stiff for birdie, Trainor drained his 60-foot putt for eagle, and a quick 1 up advantage. Trainor shot a very respectable one under par 35 on the front nine only to find himself 1 down to Haverstick's impressive outgoing 34. The match went back and forth, until a birdie at 16 put Trainor one up, and seemingly in control. On the 18th Trainor needed only a two-putt par for the win, but three-putted sending the match to the 19th hole. Now back on the par-5, 1st, Trainor "showed the gallery his opening hole eagle was no fluke." Once again he got home in two, this time sinking a 40-footer for eagle sending Haverstick on his way via the Lancaster Pike.

Future major championship winners Gay Brewer Jr. and Dow Finsterwald played in the Amateur at Saucon Valley. Philadelphia golf legends William Hyndman III, Harold Cross Jr., and W.B. "Duff" McCullough Jr. also played. The list just goes on and on.

A number of widely known figures graced the gallery both during practice rounds and championship week. Obviously, all the icons of Bethlehem Steel Corporation were present and accounted for. The championship's Honorary Chairman Eugene Grace, General Chairman Norborne Berkeley, V.J. "Pat" Pazzetti, J.J. Somerville, R. H. Schlottman, and club president W. H. Johnstone were all in attendance.

Golf royalty was represented as well. Johnny Farrell, Head Professional at the Baltusrol Golf Club in Springfield, New Jersey, was spotted in the gallery. Farrell once won six consecutive professional tournaments, but was probably best known for his victory over Bobby Jones in the 1928 U.S. Open held at Olympia Fields Country Club near Chicago. Farrell secured his victory over Jones by sinking a slippery 10-foot birdie putt on the final green of a 36 hole playoff.

Also observed admiring the play of his former rivals was 1947 U.S. Amateur champion Robert "Skee" Riegel of nearby Bucks County, Pennsylvania. Riegel turned professional in 1950, and enjoyed a brief, yet successful career as a touring professional with seven wins to his credit. At the 1951 Masters

Riegel finished in second place two strokes behind winner Ben Hogan.

There are other interesting contestants worth mentioning -- Robert Goldwater from Phoenix, was the younger brother of future presidential candidate and longtime U.S. Senator from Arizona, Barry Goldwater. Bob Goldwater was famous in his own right. In 1939 he was personally responsible for reorganizing a discontinued golf tournament in his home town. Today he is affectionately referred to as "the father of the Phoenix Open."

Ben Hogan's older brother, Royal, a 41 year-old office supply executive from Ft. Worth, also played in the U.S. Amateur at Saucon Valley. The Hogan brothers were very close. Ben's affectionate nickname for Royal was "Bubba." According to Billy Maxwell "Royal Hogan looked and dressed just like his brother." People would regularly mistake Royal for his famous sibling, and according to published reports he spent most of the week at Saucon Valley explaining he *wasn't* Ben Hogan. For those who witnessed Royal Hogan's first round loss to Thomas Sheehan of Birmingham, Michigan, no explanation was necessary. "Bubba" was 12 over par through 15, and lost 5 and 3.

There were a couple interesting travel stories reported. Bo Wininger, who needed to navigate only 100 miles from nearby Northfield, New Jersey, got lost no fewer than three times on his way to Bethlehem. Hilario Polo, an alternate from Guatemala, had a few more miles to cover on his trip. Hilario missed his connecting flight out of New Orleans and apparently misunderstood his travel options. Told a bus would leave before the next plane—he chose the bus. He arrived at Saucon Valley 52 hours later. Head Pro Ralph Hutchinson felt sorry for the Latin champion, and offered him a place to sleep immediately upon arrival, but true to his competitive creed Polo emphatically replied "No, I play golf first!"

The course would officially open to contestants on Tuesday, September 4th, with practice continuing through Sunday, September 9th. There were several thousand spectators on hand each day. In one of his practice rounds the size of Frank Stranahan's gallery was reported at over 3,000. Patrons got their money's worth as some spectacular golf was witnessed. Walker Cupper Robert Knowles of Brookline, Massachusetts, shot 67 and 69 in practice. Dick Chapman shot a pair of 67's, and Arizona's Mr. Golf, Bob Goldwater, fired five sub-par rounds, including two 67's.

The best round of the week, however, was produced by home-town favorite Jimmy McHale, who fired a course record 65. As previously mentioned, McHale wasn't afraid to shoot low numbers. His record-breaking round included a six birdie 29 on the back nine. McHale hoped playing on his home course would give him an advantage. Having never advanced past the quarterfinals in a U.S. Amateur, the talented McHale, 35, felt this was the year he would break through. During the summer leading up to the Amateur, McHale prepared for the championship by playing Saucon Valley at least three times per week. The only break from this routine occurred when he competed in the Walker Cup matches, held at the Royal Birkdale Golf Club in Great Britain. McHale even skipped playing in the U.S. Open that summer in order to concentrate on the U.S. Amateur. "I'm going to give it all I can," he said. McHale went on to emphasize he was paying particular attention to his short game, "More or less a weak spot," as he described it.

On Friday, September 7th, an informal match was held between the U.S. Walker Cup team and a team representing the Royal Canadian Golf Association. Defending champion Sam Urzetta and Frank Stranahan turned in the best individual performance. Urzetta defeated Canadian Amateur champion Walter McElroy 2 and 1. For the benefit of the large gallery

Urzetta finished out his round knocking his approach on the par-4 18th to five inches for birdie and a 1-under par round of 70. Stranahan would make a dramatic birdie on the final hole in his match against Nick Weslock to shoot even par and win 1 up. Taking a commanding 3 to 1 lead after the morning foursomes matches, the American squad would take all but one singles match in the afternoon winning the competition by the score of 10 to 2.

USA vs. CANADA

Saucon Valley Country Club
September 7, 1951

FOURSOMES

Alan Boes-Gerry Kesselring vs. Richard
Chapman-Robert Knowles 3 & 1
Don Doe-Laurie Roland vs. Sam Urzetta-Harold Paddock 4 & 3
Phil Farley-Nick Weslock vs. Charlie Coe-James McHale 2 & 1
1-up W. Mawhinney-W. McElroy vs. William Campbell-Frank Stranahan

USA 3 CANADA 1

SINGLES

Laurie Roland vs. William Campbell 4 & 3
Nick Weslock vs. Frank Stranahan 2-up
Gerry Kesselring vs. Charlie Coe 3 & 2
Phil Farley vs. James McHale 3 & 2
W. McElroy vs. Sam Urzetta 2 & 1
Don Doe vs. Harold Paddock 5 & 3
4 & 3 Alan Boes vs. Robert Knowles
W. Mawhinney vs. Richard Chapman 2-up

USA 7 CANADA 1

FINAL SCORE

USA 10 CANADA 2

CHAPTER EIGHT

Rhapsody in Blue

"An intense anticipation itself transforms possibility into reality; our desires being often but precursors of the things which we are capable of performing."

Samuel Smiles

To say the Lehigh Valley was buzzing with excitement over hosting the U.S. Amateur would be a gross understatement. Beginning with practice round week the *Bethlehem Globe-Times* gave the tournament front page coverage. U.S. Amateur headlines trumped President Truman and the United Nations.

Reporter Marie Belgrash, turned fashion editor, even got into the act:

> *"Plenty of razzle dazzle at the Saucon Valley Country Club, both on and off the golf course. Not even Jim Demaret, the number one style setting golf pro, would stand out in this crowd of spectators that are a boon to technicolor movie men."*

Belgrash went on to describe the brightly-colored clothing worn by some tournament goers as a "Rhapsody in Blue," and "Twenty shades of green." "Eye-twitching flowered shirts" roamed the fairways as well.

The price of admission for practice rounds was $1.20 daily, with a practice week pass available for $10.00. Tournament round tickets were $2.50 daily. Semifinal and final match tickets were priced at $3.50 per day. With proper introduction a clubhouse pass could be purchased for $1.00. The food in the clubhouse was not only fabulous but also affordable. Soup was 15 cents and main courses ran from $1.10 to $1.75. The highest price meal was the buffet supper which went for $3.00.

Billy Maxwell recalls the weather being pleasant but warm. Many of the contestants stayed at the Hotel Bethlehem, with some of the younger players housed at Colonial Hall at nearby Moravian College. A single room "with running water" at the Hotel Bethlehem could be had for $3.25 per day. In all, 40 contestants and eight members of the press took advantage of the free lodging at the college. The eventual semi-finalists were all living together at the dormitory. Having just lost in his own club championship at Winged Foot, Joe Gagliardi thought so little of his chances to advance in the championship he didn't make a hotel reservation, thereby ending up in Colonial Hall with Billy and the others. Cots were located throughout the locker room facilities for the player's convenience. It was going to be a long week and rest was essential. Including practice rounds, Billy would play over eleven rounds of golf in seven days.

In his introduction to the five volume photographic history of the 51st U.S. Amateur Championship, Jim White explains the outside world knew very little about Saucon Valley in 1951. It was a "mystic Camelot somewhere in Pennsylvania." That summer the excitement and anticipation for the U.S. Amateur was at an all-time high. The golfing world was about to see that Saucon Valley was truly a real place. The word quickly spread throughout the amateur golf community resulting in a large number of contestants, including the Walker Cup team, arriving early to take advantage of the full week of practice. Many of the top names played every day during the week leading up to the championship. This bonus week of excellent golf was well received by Lehigh Valley golf fans, but proved a poor strategy on the part of some contestants. Replete with upsets, the first round bloodbath continued beyond the first day, with several pre-tournament favorites playing the role of victim. Already exhausted from a full week of practice, many a famous name departed Bethlehem earlier than expected.

CHAPTER NINE

Kris Kringle Bounced in the Christmas City

"Never break your putter and your driver in the same round or you're dead."

Tommy Bolt

The opening match of the championship teed off at 7:30 a.m. on Monday, September 10th, and featured John Ward of Clay, New York, versus Edward "Kris" Kringle, of Sacramento, California. Ward won 2 and 1, prompting a slew of clever comments in the press. One scribe noted it was entirely appropriate for a "representative of Santa Claus to lead off the proceedings in the Christmas City." Another noted, "Mr. Clay showed no respect, and out Kris went."

Among the notable upsets in round one was Bill Hyndman's 2 and 1 loss to Arthur Olfs of Birmingham, Michigan. After the match Hyndman remembers witnessing a less than memorable tee shot while walking past the first tee on his way to the parking lot. Hyndman lamented, "This guy just dribbled the ball, and I said to myself why couldn't have I drawn this guy." The unknown player who topped his drive on the first hole turned out to be Joe Gagliardi, who recovered nicely from his first tee gaffe to make it all the way to the finals.

Another upset involved Lloyd Ribner over Bill Campbell. The demise of "Big Bill" Campbell was described the next morning by Ralph Bernstein writing for the Associated Press:

> *"Bill Campbell at lunch commented "this was the type of tournament, and course that might see the top boys falling like ten pins." He walked out the door, and was almost slaughtered by Lloyd Ribner of White Plains, New York 4 and 2. At one point Ribner was 5 up."*

The most notable exit in the first round, however, was that of pre-tournament favorite Frank Stranahan of Toledo, Ohio. Frankie, as he was fondly referred, found himself on the losing end of an extra holes match against little known Robert Kuntz, a 29 year-old marketing administrator from Larchmont, New York.

Stranahan, the 29 year-old heir to the Champion Spark Plug fortune, got off to a wild start---sinking a 127-foot birdie putt on the first green. Rick McCall, a ten year-old schoolboy at the time, recalls tournament officials later measuring the distance of the putt. Stranahan continued his solid play and arrived at the 17th tee dormie (two up with two holes to play). It was at this point in the match events made a dramatic turn in favor of Kuntz. Kuntz won the 17th with a birdie after a beautiful approach to two feet. Still hanging by a thread after his birdie on 17, Kuntz evened the match by dropping his 8-foot birdie putt on the 18th. Despite Stranahan's status as gallery favorite, Kuntz received a rousing ovation from more than 2,000 spectators surrounding the 18th green.

The magic continued on the first playoff hole, with Kuntz recording his third birdie in a row matching Stranahan's great up and down bird from the greenside bunker. At the 20th Stranahan missed the green short left, failed to save par, and Kuntz, a self-proclaimed weekend golfer competing in the first match play event of his career, advanced to the next round!

Kuntz's wife, Doris, wept tears of joy once victory was assured. "I knew he'd do it," she exclaimed. "I knew Bob was going to win when he took the 17th hole to cut the lead to one hole." Surrounded by several members of the press, the pretty brunette went on to explain, "I could feel it in my bones that he'd tie the match on the 18th and then win it in one of the extra holes. Did you ever just get a feeling that something was inevitable? That's how I felt."

The stunning upset of Stranahan, also known as "The Toledo Strongman," because of his stringent physical fitness regimen, caused fear among golf correspondents that a "hacker" might end up the national amateur champion! Of course, in the end those concerns proved unfounded as talent always seems to find its way to the top. Although he accepted the loss as a true sportsman, there was little consolation for Stranahan, who had spent the previous two weeks in Texas honing his game under the watchful eye of Ben Hogan. This marked the ninth time the talented Stranahan experienced disappointment at the national championship. He was runner-up to Urzetta the previous year, losing on the 39th hole in what is still a record for the longest finals match in U.S. Amateur history.

Located in the 1951 Championship file at the USGA Library is a handwritten note documenting Frank Stranahan's disappointment for letting down one of his fans:

> *"Joseph Littlefield from Chicago drove all the way to Saucon Valley to watch Frank play. Frank lost to Bob Kuntz in the first round. Clubs over his shoulder Frank met Mr. Littlefield in the hotel lobby, and had to tell him 'Mr. Littlefield, it breaks my heart to tell you I lost today in the first round.' Frankie went on to say, 'Mr. L was a real golf fan. I felt sorry that he came that far. That he took time off from his work. Made me feel even sadder than just losing.'"*

In his next match versus Wynsol Spencer of Newport News, Virginia, Kuntz would once again make a "mad dash" at the finish to force overtime. Three down with three to play, Kuntz would win the 16th with a birdie, 17 with par, and another birdie at 18 would square the match against Spencer. Luck would finally run out on Kuntz on the 19th, however, as his 4-foot birdie try would "rim the cup," sending him back to the office.

As is the case in all tournaments played at match play there were still plenty of surprises ahead. For example, the entire Walker Cup delegation was picked off, one by one, until, like the nursery rhyme says, "then there were none." In his first round match, Walker Cupper Robert Knowles, one of several pre-tournament favorites, was upset by underdog Robert Eckis Jr. of Williamsville, New York. Eckis' previous "claim to fame" was he once won a golf tournament when he was 10 years old. Ralph Bernstein wrote, "What famous golf head will roll next?"

One of the biggest eye-openers could best be described as the Saucon Valley Black Out. On the back nine during his fourth round match, Sam Urzetta was cruising along with a 4 up lead over Joe Gagliardi when, as they say in the business, the wheels came off. Urzetta proceeded to lose six of the next eight holes. He lost five in a row, and during that stretch of holes he made only one par. "I blacked out... I didn't know where my shots were going off the tee," explained Urzetta. Urzetta was attempting to become the first repeat winner since Lawson Little won back to back championships in 1934-35. The former St. Bonaventure basketball star, and lumber salesman, could be heard 30 minutes after the match asking the question, "Anyone want to buy some lumber?" His sense of humor inspired a correspondent to write he was witness to "The death of an Amateur champion and the rebirth of a salesman."

While his gregarious opponent held court, Gagliardi, quietly, and methodically, advanced closer to his place in history by the margin of 2 and 1.

OFFICIAL SCORECARD

51st Amateur Championship of The United States Golf Association

Saucon Valley Country Club, Bethlehem, Pennsylvania
September 10-15, 1951

Official Yardage and Par

Hole		*Yards	Par	Hole		*Yards	Par
1	-	516	5	10	-	403	4
2	-	405	4	11	-	187	3
3	-	385	4	12	-	433	4
4	-	175	3	13	-	352	4
5	-	437	4	14	-	203	3
6	-	586	5	15	-	612	5
7	-	446	4	16	-	448	4
8	-	389	4	17	-	437	4
9	-	193	3	18	-	372	4
____		____	____	____		____	____
OUT		3,532	36	IN		3,447	35

TOTAL YARDS - 6,979

TOTAL PAR - 71

*Measured from 2 yards from rear of tee to 5 yards from rear of green

CHAPTER TEN

Stymie

"The greater the obstacle, the more glory in overcoming it."

Moliere

The 51st U.S. Amateur Championship at Saucon Valley would be conducted under the strict rules of the USGA, except where modified by local rules. One local rule in 1951 identified both out of bounds and water hazards by white stakes. "Large" white stakes signified out of bounds while "small" white stakes marked water hazards.

White stakes would remain the designated manner for identifying out of bounds in the future, but in order to avoid confusion, water hazards and lateral water hazards would later be identified by yellow and red stakes respectively.

There were two very interesting stipulations to the Rules of Amateur Status in effect for the 1951 U.S. Amateur. The first involved athletic scholarships. It was impermissible because of golf skill or reputation to accept a scholarship as an inducement to be a student in an institution of learning. An exception to this rule was if the scholarship was won as a prize in a recognized golf competition, and received prior to the player's eighteenth birthday. Under this exception the scholarship was allowed even though the period of the award extended beyond the eighteenth birthday.

Another violation of Amateur Status in 1951 was accepting compensation as a Caddie, Caddie-Master, or Assistant Caddie-Master after the 21st birthday. Considering a Caddie, or Caddie-Master, a professional, is rooted in golf's cultural history. In golf's early years, Golf Professionals were not allowed to use clubhouse facilities and were even prohibited from entering the clubhouse by the front door. Caddies and Golf Professionals were once considered in the same social class.

The "turning point" came at the 1920 U.S. Open in Toledo, Ohio. The players, encouraged by professional Walter Hagen, donated a large grandfather clock to the host Inverness Club in appreciation for the club allowing access to the clubhouse by the professionals during the tournament.

The prohibition of athletic scholarships for golf was modified in 1953 and removed completely in 1960 with the NCAA named in the code. The violation for working as a Caddie, Caddie-Master or Assistant Caddie-Master, was dropped from the code completely in 1963.

An archaic, yet very interesting, rule of golf still in effect for the Amateur championship at Saucon Valley was the "stymie."

Webster's defines stymie as "to present an obstacle to," or "to stand in the way of."

Writing in *The Golf Dictionary*, Michael Corcoran explains, "stymie describes a situation in match play wherein one player's ball blocked another's path to the hole. The only remedy for the player whose path was blocked (stymied) was to putt around or chip over the intruding ball, known as jumping a stymie."

"A stymie was only possible in match play involving one ball per side, and both balls involved must be at least six inches apart. If the nearer ball is struck there is no penalty. However, the opponent has the option of either playing the ball as it lies or replacing it. If the nearer ball is knocked into the hole, then the opponent is deemed to have holed out with his previous stroke."

In order to serve as a method of measurement the official scorecard for the championship was manufactured six inches wide. "Stymie Measure – Six Inches" was printed across the bottom of every official scorecard used in the 1951 U.S. Amateur.

Due to the abundance of stroke play competition in the United States and the considerable element of chance, the stymie was never widely popular. Despite this, Bobby Jones, and five-time Open Champion J.H. Taylor, remained staunch supporters of the stymie. It was Jones who went on record in support of maintaining the stymie. In an impassioned letter to the USGA, Jones, in part, made the following point:

> *"More than anything else it points to the value of always being closer to the hole on the shot to the green and after the first putt."*

Despite an endorsement from the greatest amateur of all time, the stymie's days were numbered. The PGA of America had already done away with the stymie in 1944. In December 1951, less than three months after the Amateur at Saucon Valley, the R&A and USGA met for the first time in a joint conference on the rules. The result of this conference was the first Unified Worldwide Code of 1952, in which the stymie was abolished.

The stymie, a relic of golf history, made its final appearance in America's national championship at Saucon Valley.

The media center at Saucon Valley Country Club, referred to as "the most palatial press headquarters in golfing history," featured special lighting and custom-built individual typewriter stations. (Photo courtesy of Saucon Valley Country Club).

Eugene Gifford Grace, Patriarch of Saucon Valley Country Club.
(Image courtesy of Saucon Valley Country Club)

Leonard Strong, Course Superintendent. Strong was the younger brother of course architect Herbert Strong.
(Photo courtesy of Saucon Valley Country Club)

Billy Maxwell, a 22 year-old college student became the second youngest U.S. Amateur champion and first champion from the state of Texas. (Photo courtesy of Saucon Valley Country Club)

Charles "Chick" Evans (left), 1916 U.S. Open and U.S. Amateur champion, with Eugene Grace. The Amateur championship at Saucon Valley marked the 42nd consecutive appearance in the U.S. Amateur for Evans. (Photo courtesy of Saucon Valley Country Club)

All the greats played in the U.S. Amateur at Saucon Valley. (From left to right) Robert Knowles, 1950 French Amateur champion; Sam Urzetta, 1950 U.S. Amateur champion; Richard Chapman, 1951 British Amateur champion. (Photo courtesy of Saucon Valley Country Club)

Tommy Jacobs, 16, 1951 U.S. Junior Amateur champion (left), poses with good friend David Stanley, 20, 1951 U. S. Amateur Public Links champion. Both young men hailed from the same home town of Montebello, California. (Photo courtesy of Saucon Valley Country Club)

Saucon Valley legend Ross "Cotton" Young caddied for Dale Morey in the 1951 U.S. Amateur. Young's career at the club spanned eight decades, and he is a member of the inaugural class of the PCA Worldwide Caddie Hall of Fame."
(Photo courtesy of Saucon Valley Country Club)

William "Dynamite" Goodloe Jr. (left) and Jim McHale Jr. discuss strategy during the 1949 Walker Cup Matches at the Winged Foot Golf Club in Mamaroneck, New York. (Photo courtesy of Saucon Valley Country Club)

Pre-tournament favorite Frank Stranahan blasts from the greenside bunker on the 18th hole of his first round match against Robert Kuntz. Kuntz would birdie the 17th and 18th holes to square the match, and eventually defeat Stranahan on the 20th hole. (Photo courtesy of Saucon Valley Country Club)

Arnold Blum of Macon, Georgia, chips from behind the 18th green in his quarter-final match versus Billy Maxwell. Blum failed to save par and lost to Maxwell on the 20th hole. (Photo courtesy of Saucon Valley Country Club)

Saucon Valley member Jim McHale Jr. (right) congratulates Billy Joe Patton after Patton's 1 up victory in their third round match. (Photo courtesy of Saucon Valley Country Club)

Semi-finalists pose with the Havemeyer Trophy. (Left to right) Joe Gagliardi, Billy Maxwell, Tommy Jacobs, John Benson. (Photo courtesy of Saucon Valley Country Club)

The scene around the 14th green following Maxwell's hole-out from the bunker during the morning round of his final match versus Joe Gagliardi. On the right side of the photo Maxwell can be seen walking off the green. (Photo courtesy of Saucon Valley Country Club)

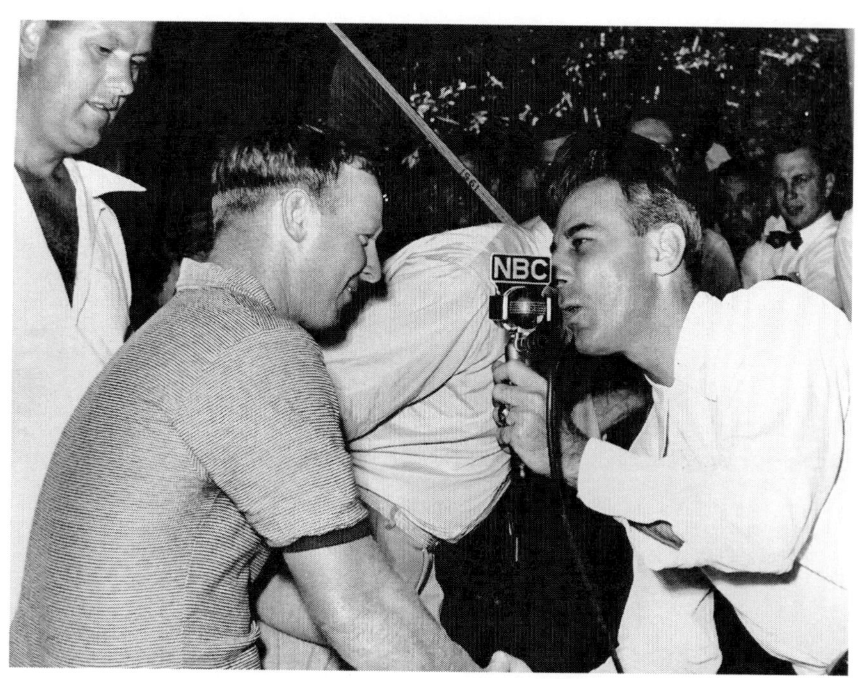

Bill Stern (right) of NBC radio congratulates Billy Maxwell immediately following his victory in the 1951 U.S. Amateur Championship. Stern's interview of Maxwell would broadcast live to a national audience. (Photo courtesy of Saucon Valley Country Club)

THE ODESSA (TEXAS) AMERICAN, SEPTEMBER 16, 1951

Maxwell Wins National Amateur

Odessan Becomes Youngest Winner Since Bob Jones

BETHLEHEM, Pa. (UP)—Sandy-haired Billy Maxwell, a tough little 22-year-old Texan, Saturday became the youngest winner of the U. S. Amateur golf championship since Bobby Jones as he defeated lawyer Joe Gagliardi, Mamoroneck, N. Y., 4 and 3.

The same age as the "emperor" was when he scored his initial triumph in 1924, the bantam battler from Odessa, won the hearts of a gallery of 7,000 in the bright sunshine which flooded Saucon Valley Country Club as he flattened his 39-year-old rival with a set of red hot irons.

Maxwell, a pre-tournament unknown even though he captains North Texas State's three-time NCAA golf champions, thus became the first fairway artist from the Lone Star state to win the national. And the chunky five-foot, seven-inch slugger did it with a precision-built game and a heart which never faltered.

Gagliardi, New York metropolitan amateur king, had been a cool customer all the way through the early rounds as he knocked off former champions Charley Coe and Sam Urzetta. And he jumped off to a one up lead over little Billy at the nine-hole mark of their 36-hole final.

But the blue-eyed kid from Texas, didn't fold. In a match where neither spoke at any time; Maxwell fought to a two up edge at 18 with a one under par 36-34—70 against Gagliardi's 36-37—73. Little Billy made it three up at 27 with a one over par 37 against a 39 and then built his advantage to four up and ran it out.

For the 33 holes required, young Billy was exactly even par while Gagliardi was six over.

The New Yorker could have alibied his defeat—but he didn't. Friday night for the second night in a row, he had three abcessed teeth lanced. The jaw pained him Saturday but he—like the almost casual youngster from the plains of West Texas—played without expression.

And there were many times when each of them might have grinned or grimaced in this pressure-packed final for America's highest amateur golfing honor. The most painful moment for swarthy Joe came on the 203-yard 14th hole in the morning round when, as they battled all even, Gagliardi hit a beautiful four wood seven feet from the pin and Mawell drove into a trap where his ball nestled in the sand 40 feet from the pin.

It looked like Gagliardi's hole. But little Billy had other ideas. Taking a lazy half-swing, he wedged the ball out, and taking two little hops, it bounced into the hole for a deuce.

Gagliardi missed his putt and went one down. That was the turning point, for never again was he able to catch the Dixie Dynamiter.

The New Yorker had gone one down on the 385-yard par four third wth a bogey as he underclubbed his approach and dropped it into a creek in front of the green. He played his fourth shot five feet from the pin, but Maxwell, only 12 feet away, stepped up and rattled the cup for a winning birdie.

Gagliardi, cool and unaffected, squared it with a birdie four on the 586-yard sixth when he knocked his third shot hole high, 25 feet away, and then rammed it home.

BILLY MAXWELL . . . Irons Were Hot

They matched shot for shot, with Gagliardi scrambling cooly, through the eighth. But then the battling barrister took the lead as Maxwell went one over par on the 193-yard par three ninth. Little Billy beat himself there by driving a trap, 70 feet from the pin, and coming out poorly to two-putt.

Turning for home, Maxwell wasn't long getting even as he won the 403-yard par four 10th with a par. Gagliardi sprayed his drive into the rough, left a three wood 100 yards short, but his approach 10 feet from the wicket, and missed the putt.

But Joe went one up again on the 187-yard 11th as he grabbed that putter and whacked in a 34-footer which made his 14-year-old son, Joe Jr.,—one of five little Gagliardis, grin in glee.

Billy, a bridegroom whose shortened finances sent him on a golfing honeymoon without his bride, stayed one down for only one hole. For his steady par on the 352-yard 13th squared it again as Gagliardi caught a trap with his second shot and took a bogey five.

Then came that sensational sand shot of Maxwell's on the 14th and, while nobody knew it at the time, that was the match.

They halved the next hole with pars but Maxwell made his margin three up by winning the 16th and 17th, both with pars.

Still the New Yorker didn't collapse. On the 372-yard par four 18th he put his second on the green and sank a 25-foot putt which left him only two down as they finished the morning 18 holes.

Starting the afternoon round, Maxwell won the 516-yard 19th with a birdie four by putting his approach four feet from the pin and sinking. He went four up taking the 405-yard 20th with a par, as Gagliardi three-putted from 50 feet—missing his second putt from four feet.

Billy went five up on the 175-yard par three 22nd hole when he knocked a six iron eight feet from the flag and dropped the birdie putt but he lost the 26th by three-putting from 40 feet and the 193-yard 27th as his drive caught a trap. Still, the Texan was three up at the turn.

Continued

On Sunday morning September 16, 1951, Billy Maxwell's victory was proclaimed in Odessa, Texas. ("Maxwell Wins National Amateur" headline story - image courtesy of *The Odessa American*)

(From left to right) Eugene Grace, Billy Maxwell, and USGA President James Standish with the Havemeyer Trophy. (Photo courtesy of Saucon Valley Country Club)

A crowd of over 1,000 remained for the awards ceremony held at the pool area. This view shows the large crowd with the clubhouse in the background. (Photo courtesy of Saucon Valley Country Club)

A massive gallery follows play on the 15th fairway during the morning round of the finals. All existing attendance records for the U.S. Amateur were broken at Saucon Valley in 1951. (Photo courtesy of Saucon Valley Country Club)

Located at the first tee of the Old Course, this plaque commemorates all champions of USGA championships held at Saucon Valley. To date, the club has played host to seven USGA championships the 1951 U.S. Amateur being the first. (Author photo)

(From left to right) William Gordon, Eugene Grace, and V.J. "Pat" Pazzetti. Gordon would go on to design both the Grace and Weyhill courses at Saucon Valley under the watchful eye of Pazzetti, long-time Green Committee Chairman. (Photo courtesy of Saucon Valley Country Club)

The Saucon Valley Country Club "brain trust," (from left to right) W.H. Johnstone, V.J. Pazzetti, Eugene Grace, Norborne Berkeley, R.H. Schlottman, and John J. Somerville. (Photo Courtesy of Saucon Valley Country Club)

Billy Maxwell meets with members of the press following his 4 & 3 triumph over Joe Gagliardi in the final match of the 1951 U.S. Amateur Championship. (Photo courtesy of Saucon Valley Country Club)

"Giant Killer of Winged Foot" versus "The West Texas Cyclone." Joe Gagliardi (left) and Billy Maxwell pose for this photograph prior to the final match of the 51st U.S. Amateur Championship at Saucon Valley Country Club. (Photo courtesy of Saucon Valley Country Club)

USGA President James Standish congratulates newly crowned U.S. Amateur champion Billy Maxwell. (Photo courtesy of Saucon Valley Country Club)

CHAPTER ELEVEN

The Seige Gun of South Hills Country Club

"One man practicing sportsmanship is far better than a hundred teaching it."

Knute Rockne

By the time Billy Maxwell arrived at Saucon Valley he had already played in over 100 golf tournaments before the age of 21. This was his second U.S. Amateur, having advanced to the round of 16 the previous year at the Minneapolis Golf Club. In 1951 there were no qualifying rounds to seed the players. All players who qualified for the championship moved right into match play. This meant 200 contestants, in four different match play brackets, requiring 74 matches to be played the first day and another 64 matches the next day. Billy found himself in the lower half of the fourth bracket with a bye in the first round. He's not sure why he had the benefit of the bye, but after several days of practice he welcomed the extra day of rest.

Billy's tournament began in the second round on Tuesday morning against Tom Strange Jr. of Cincinnati, Ohio. Billy's first opponent, excuse the pun, was no stranger to top flight competition. Despite being only 20 years of age, Strange had already played in three U.S. Opens (1949-1951). Tom Strange was a very tough opponent, but Billy got off to a great start, and prevailed by the score of 2 and 1. This marked the second year in a row the talented Strange failed to advance past the second round in the U.S. Amateur. In 1950 at Minneapolis he lost a "nail biter" on the final hole to Raymond Watson of Kansas City.

Tom Strange went on to have an extremely successful career as a PGA Professional in the Mid-Atlantic region. In addition to being one of the country's finest players, he became a highly regarded teacher as well. Tom's most famous student was his own son, two-time U.S. Open champion Curtis Strange.

Bragging rights between Tom Strange, and Ray Watson, are left for the reader to decide. Ray also had a son who took up the game---eight-time major championship winner Tom Watson.

It was now Wednesday, and with the third round of match play about to commence there had still been no mention of Billy Maxwell in the press. Buried in the last line of the last page of that day's issue of the Bethlehem Globe-Times was the following:

> *"Billy Maxwell, Southern Collegiate Champion from North Texas State. This 22 year- old hits them long and accurate and could cause a lot of trouble."*

In the morning match Billy faced Francis G. "Bo" Wininger of Oklahoma (State) A&M. Wininger, a WW II Navy veteran, played on the same high school football and baseball teams in Commerce, Oklahoma, as the great Mickey Mantle, although a few years ahead of the future Yankee slugger. Billy dispatched the talented Wininger 2 up. Bo went on to win the 1953 Pennsylvania Open and enjoyed a successful, although short career on the PGA Tour. At the 1955 Baton Rouge Open Bo Wininger squared the match, so to speak, when he won his first PGA Tour event in a playoff --- against Billy Maxwell.

That afternoon Billy squared off against E. Harvie Ward of Fayetteville, North Carolina. According to former New Jersey and Philadelphia Amateur Champion Bill McGuinness, a student of Ward's in the early 1990's, Ward possessed "Hollywood good looks and an even better personality." His golf game was even more impressive. In 1951 Ward was considered the best amateur player in the country. Ward had narrowly escaped defeat in the previous round against a surprising John Humm of Rockville Center, New York. The dramatic highlight of the match occurred on the 18th green with Ward 1 up. Ward laid a perfect stymie on Humm about two feet from the hole. From four feet away Humm proceeded to chip over Ward's ball and into the cup for par. Confronted with a relatively short left to right breaking putt Ward slipped it in on the low side for the victory.

Billy played his best golf of the championship against Ward. Harvie Ward would shoot two under par on the front nine only to find himself 2 down to Maxwell's brilliant outgoing 32. Undaunted, Ward would not go down without a fight. He reduced the margin to one hole at the 13th by holing out from the fairway for eagle. Ward's spectacular shot wasn't enough, as the constant grind of playing from behind finally began to take its toll resulting in bogies on 15 and 16, and as Bud Weiser of the *Allentown Morning Call* reported, "That was it." Billy defeated the best amateur in America by a score of 3 and 2. Incredibly, the win over Ward was reported in the press as "A mild upset by a virtual unknown, Billy Maxwell of Texas." Most of the attention was still focused on other players.

The third round match between Walker Cup teammates, Jimmy McHale and Billy Joe Patton, generated a great deal of interest. A gallery of several thousand followed as heavyweights McHale and Patton exchanged blows all the way to the final hole. Forging an impressive 4 up lead after 11 holes, Patton appeared to have McHale against the ropes. However, Patton found bunker trouble on 12 and 13, allowing McHale to close the gap to two holes. McHale came back with a 15-foot birdie on 14, and then won the 15th with a par to even the match. McHale found trouble off the tee on 16, losing the hole to Patton's par. Both players parred the 17th, setting up the dramatic finish. On the 18th Patton drove long and left into the heavy rough, while McHale blistered his drive down the middle. Patton hit a tremendous wedge shot to within 8 feet. McHale responded with an equally great shot finishing 10 feet above the hole. With the pressure on, McHale gently stroked the slick right to left breaking putt into the middle of the hole. Patton would now need to make his putt to avoid going extra holes. Equal to the occasion, Billy Joe calmly stepped up and canned the 8-footer, sending Saucon Valley's favorite son packing 1 up. Later, in a personal note to tournament officials, Jim McHale summed up his feelings on playing the national championship on his home course:

> *"I have played in many championships since starting my golfing career but I want to say that the one at Saucon Valley is the finest I have ever competed in. My only regret being that I could not keep the cup at Saucon Valley."*

Billy remembers being exhausted after his matches versus Wininger and Ward. "They were equally good players, and that took something out of me," he recalled. He would need a good night's sleep, because the next day would be a marathon. Billy would play more holes on Thursday than anyone else in the field.

Next up, in the fifth round, would be Billy's North Texas State teammate, and reigning Trans-Miss Amateur champion, L.M. Crannell Jr. of Dallas. Having just defeated Dick Chapman in the previous round, Crannell was at the top of his game. The familiar competitors fought back and forth. Bob Harlow reported both players were "hugging par" the entire match. Crannell was 1 up with 3 to play when Billy rammed in a 40-footer at the 16th for birdie to even the match. Both parred 17 and 18, sending the match to extra holes. Billy prevailed on the 19th with a par, after Crannell uncharacteristically three-putted.

Advancing to the quarterfinals, Billy would face, yet again, a very strong opponent in Arnold Blum of Macon, Georgia. Blum, a lifelong amateur, had won the SEC Championship in 1941 while at the University of Georgia. Blum would go on to win the Georgia Amateur five times and play on a victorious Walker Cup Team. He also played in the Masters five times, and in 1989, along with Bobby Jones, would be inducted into the inaugural class of the Georgia Golf Hall of Fame.

"In the quarterfinals I was playing the boy from Georgia. He really should have beat me," Billy explained. Going back and forth the match would finish even after the first nine holes. Bud Weiser of the *Allentown Morning Call* reported, "On the 10th green Billy would give Blum a rather rare assist." In what was described as "the most unusual shot of the week," Blum, lying two, 7 feet from the hole, laid a perfect stymie on Billy, who was 12 feet away on the same line. Billy attempted to putt around the stymie, but inadvertently hit Blum's ball into the hole. By rule, Blum was considered holed out with his previous stroke, thereby winning the hole with an eagle 2. Blum made it

2 up after a birdie on 12, gave one back with a 6 on 13, then won 14 with a par. Billy won the 16th with a par, narrowing the margin to one. After halving the 17th they came to the final hole with Blum still 1 up. Both players found the fairway with their drives on the 18th. What happened next was inexplicable, or as Francis Ouimet once explained, "Anything can happen in golf, and usually does." Billy describes the action, "I was one down with one to play. Blum bladed that 9 iron over the green. There were so many people...they parted like the Red Sea and the ball went over the green!" It took Blum three to get down from behind the green, and for the second time that day Billy would head to extra holes.

Perhaps still in a state of disbelief, Billy struggled on the 19th. Looking at what would be his most important putt of the championship, Billy gathered himself just in time to make the 14-footer for par, forcing Blum to sink his putt from four feet for the tie. On the 20th, Billy's second shot finished 15 feet from the hole in the fringe. Blum's ball found the green, but was on the opposite side of the large hump 45 feet away. Blum's first putt barely made it over the rise in the green and finished well short. After missing his next putt he conceded Billy's short putt for par.

Blum would continue to have a very successful amateur career. However, it was the 1952 U.S. Amateur at the Seattle Golf Club where Arnold Blum would unknowingly play a significant role in golf history. In a personal letter to fan John F. Gleason Jr. dated November 23, 1992, golf legend Ken Venturi writes:

> *"I really only played in two U.S. Amateurs. In 1952 I lost in the 1st round. I was three down and four to go to Arnold Blum. I birdied 15-16-17; he birdied 18 to win. If I hadn't lost, I would never have met and worked with Byron Nelson."*

His hard fought victory over Blum in the quarters earned Billy a spot in the semifinals versus dark horse John Benson of Pittsburgh. He also found himself in an interesting predicament. He had no clothes to wear! Billy arrived at Saucon Valley with one pair of pants, not because he packed only one pair--- he only owned one pair. He brought along several shirts, but not expecting to make it this far into the tournament he completely ran out of clean clothes. Jim White, whose father Daniel White was the Club Manager at the time tells the story, "Billy was in the habit of sitting on the front steps of the clubhouse as a means of relaxation in between rounds." White continues, "It was during these times my dad would chat with Billy, and during one of these conversations he learned Billy had no clean clothes left. So my dad had all of Billy's clothes washed in the club laundry."

John Benson found himself in a similar situation but for different reasons. Benson brought only a small overnight bag to Saucon Valley. After two days he was out of clothes but solved his problem in a different manner. Benson purchased a new wardrobe from the pro shop each day. In a photograph appearing in the *Bethlehem Globe-Times*, Benson and his fellow semifinalists are shown posing with the Havemeyer Trophy. A close inspection of the photo reveals the pant leg of Benson's slacks turned up. Benson bought a new pair each day, and didn't have time for the slacks to be properly hemmed.

In a match featuring the two youngest remaining players, 16 year-old Tommy Jacobs defeated 19 year-old Billy Picard 1 up. Picard was one down at the turn, but drew even after a birdie at the par-3 14th hole. Both players parred the next three holes. On 18 Picard found trouble off the tee and was bunkered on his second. Picard was unable to get up and down and Jacobs advanced.

Picard, a pre-law student at Citadel University, expressed no intention of following in the footsteps of his famous father. "A fellow ought to have something to fall back on," he said. Billy learned the game from his father, golf professional Henry Picard. In addition to winning the Masters and PGA championship, Henry Picard was a highly respected teacher. Another of Picard's pupils was Ben Hogan. It was Picard, who in the late 1930's recommended Hogan weaken his grip. In appreciation for the career changing advice, Hogan dedicated his first book, <u>Power Golf</u>, to Picard in 1953.

Jacobs would next face Ed Martin, the Massachusetts Amateur champion. Tommy dispatched "Big Ed" by an impressive margin of 5 and 4. With his win over Martin, Jacobs became the youngest player in 47 years to advance to the semifinals of the U.S. Amateur. "I was supposed to be in school last Monday," he laughed after his win over Martin. "Every day I win is another day off from school, but I don't think the truant officer will be here after me...I'm not particularly worried. I've got a little pull," Tommy explained. Fortunately for Jacobs his high school Principal was an avid golfer and one of his biggest supporters.

While Jacobs advanced past the veteran Martin, 1951 Metropolitan Amateur Champion Joe Gagliardi (pronounced Gal-Yard-Di) of the Winged Foot Golf Club was taking on 1949 Amateur champion Charlie Coe. Winged Foot's widely known professional, Claude Harmon, flew in from New York the night before in order to watch Gagliardi play on Thursday.

The afternoon match between Gagliardi and Coe would attract a gallery of 5,000. The huge crowd was treated to a great match between two equally great players. Normally known for his consistent ball striking ability, on this occasion Gagliardi spent most of the match making incredible par saves with a dazzling display of the short game. The match went back and forth, with Coe consistently outdriving Gagliardi by 50 yards, but unable to cash in on his advantage off the tee. Gagliardi was making putts from everywhere. Coe finally appeared in position to win on the 16th, only to see Gagliardi sink yet another 12-footer for the half. It was at this point Coe succumbed to the persistent pressure. With Gagliardi's drive in the middle of the 17th fairway, Coe snap-hooked his tee shot across the creek and near the 16th fairway. With no shot to the green, Coe lost the 17th to Gagliardi's routine two-putt par. On the 18th Coe hit what was described as "one of the worst shots seen in the tourney." The 1949 Amateur champion heeled his drive and struck a tree no more than 50 yards from the tee. Coe took two more to get to the green, and when his fourth wasn't even close, he conceded the match to Gagliardi.

Charlie Coe recovered from the loss to Joe Gagliardi and continued to star on golf's national and international stage. He would win a second U.S. Amateur title in 1958 and was runner-up to Jack Nicklaus in 1959. Coe played on six Walker Cup teams. He played in the Masters 19 times and holds virtually every Masters amateur record. His best finish at Augusta was runner-up to Gary Player in 1961.

John Benson was probably the only semifinalist who woke up that Friday morning wondering how he got there. At 6 foot 2 inches and 228 pounds Benson was known to his friends as "Big Jack." He had also earned the title "Siege Gun of South Hills Country Club" due to his awe-inspiring length off the tee. Benson was no doubt an excellent player. He defeated Gay Brewer in the 4th round and followed up that victory with the upset of Harold Paddock Jr. in round 5. By his own admission he was at Saucon Valley merely as a diversion from everyday life. Big Jack had not played in the national championship since 1935, and said he only entered the tournament "...to get away from the multitudinous noises the four children make around the home."

In describing Benson's upset of Paddock Bob Harlow of _Golf World_ penned the following editorial:

> *"How Benson beat Paddock nobody knows, but he did it. No reflection is implied here about Mr. Benson. But Harold Paddock is a noted match play golfer who has won the Ohio state twice, has as good a "staying" record as any player in the national amateur in recent years and was considered good enough to make the Walker Cup team. No competent critic would expect Benson to beat Paddock. The answer must be---that's golf!"*

Three up after 10, Benson seemed in total control of his match with Paddock. Using a putter with an unusual bend in the shaft, Benson required only seven putts on the front nine. The story behind his unique putter goes like this ---once upon a time in a fit of anger Benson threw his putter against a tree. The result was a putter with a pronounced bend in the shaft. Embarrassed by this temporary act of insanity, Benson decided an appropriate punishment would be to continue using this same putter for the remainder of the round. To his surprise he putted brilliantly with the damaged club. As a result, all his future putters were customized with this same bend in the shaft.

Several years later, in response to Karsten Solheim's popular Ping putter with a similar feature, the USGA would ban all clubs with a bend in the shaft higher than 5 inches from the club head.

Paddock's birdie at the 11th reduced the margin to two. After Benson made consecutive bogeys on 15 and 16, the match was all square. Both players made routine pars on the 17th setting up the closing hole drama. On the 18th Benson lived up to his reputation by unleashing a drive an incredible 350 yards, with the ball coming to rest just below the green. Benson chipped to 3 feet for the easy birdie, and a stunning upset over the highly regarded Paddock.

In the afternoon Benson took early control of his quarterfinal match versus James Frisina of Springfield, Illinios. He was two under par on the front nine and 4 up. He remained 4 up with three to play to earn his spot in the semifinal versus Billy. Benson stayed around longer than he, or anyone else, had anticipated. A credit to his competitive spirit, Big Jack would not be denied. That is, until he met "The West Texas Cyclone."

The semifinal and final matches would both be contested over 36 holes. It was late in the week. Fatigue was no doubt beginning to take a toll on the competitors. Billy, however, seemed just as fresh as his newly laundered attire. Benson, on the other hand, was a different player in the semifinals. Overshooting greens and shanking irons, he couldn't get anything going and fell behind early. The long week of competition finally began to show on the 40 year-old father of four. When his game started going sideways (literally), Benson was unable to make up any ground on Billy, who never strayed from par all week. Billy was 7 up after the morning round, having shot a medal score of 73 to Benson's 80. Billy would go on to win three of the last five holes to claim victory by the lopsided margin of 10 and 9. The match ended on the 27th hole, symbolically within walking distance of the First-Aid station. Good natured in defeat, Big Jack was observed late in the abbreviated match retrieving a small container from his golf bag in order to "partake of the flask of encouragement."

As the Benson-Maxwell match ended on the 9th green, the skies opened. Playing ahead on their 28th hole, Tommy Jacobs and Joe Gagliardi would need to play the final few holes in a driving rain.

Already 5 up when the rain began to fall, Gagliardi continued to display "a mastery of the trouble shot." On the 31st he found two bunkers but still managed a par to clinch the victory. Judge Joe won by the impressive score of 6 and 5, needing only 21 putts in the morning round and finishing the match at even par. The only time Jacobs was all-square was on the first hole, and after the 5th he was never better than 2 down.

Tommy Jacobs would go on to enjoy a successful career on the PGA Tour. He would later become a highly respected instructor, but not before he established a record for being the youngest person to ever play in the Masters. Jacobs would hold this distinction for 58 years until Matteo Manassero broke his record in 2010.

While Billy needed to navigate the most difficult half of the most difficult quarter of the draw, Gagliardi had earned the moniker "Giant Killer" for his impressive wins over several quality players, including defending champion Sam Urzetta, Charlie Coe, and 1940 U.S. Amateur runner-up "Duff" McCullough of Philadelphia. The story line for the finals would be Maxwell's youth versus the experience of Joe Gagliardi.

Billy Maxwell had risen from obscurity to headline in a matter of two days.

CHAPTER TWELVE

The West Texas Cyclone vs. Giant Killer of Winged Foot

"The most rewarding things you do in life are the ones that look like they cannot be done."

Arnold Palmer

Although the weather for Saturday's final match was beautiful, the downpour the previous afternoon and evening left the golf course very wet, and it played even longer than the advertised yardage of 6,979. With Gagliardi unable to reach 16 or 17 in regulation the conditions seemed to favor a younger Maxwell. Gagliardi, a 39 year-old attorney and New York District Justice, resorted to using a portable seat in order to preserve precious energy during the final. The USGA issued Gagliardi's oldest son, 14 year-old Joe Jr. a Marshall credential in order for him to carry the seat for his father.

Exhaustion wasn't the only challenge facing Gagliardi. Earlier in the week he had undergone an emergency dental procedure on three abscessed teeth. His doctor indicated the pain was so severe Gagliardi hadn't eaten a full meal in days. Despite being "pumped full of medicine" and enduring significant discomfort, Gagliardi never complained. Rising above the adversity he managed to keep his ball in the fairway, while Billy struggled early to find the short grass. However, it wasn't long before Billy settled in, and returned to what Lincoln Werden, writing in *The New YorkTimes*, called "unbeatable golf." His accurate drives and precise approaches "moved across the Saucon Valley landscape like a well-oiled machine." The national media had now discovered Billy Maxwell, and like their counterparts in Texas, looked upon Billy's dominating performance and drew similar comparisons to Lone Star state golfers' Ben Hogan and Byron Nelson.

Although he holed a 30-foot birdie putt on the 18th to win the final hole of the morning round, Gagliardi was never able to get closer than 2 down to Maxwell, who had played the first 18 holes one-under par.

The atmosphere for the finals was electric. The gallery was estimated at 7,000 spectators. A new attendance record for the U.S. Amateur was established with the vast crowds surpassing the previous mark set at Merion in 1930, the year Bobby Jones completed the Grand Slam. Local radio station WGPA carried the action throughout the day on Saturday. "Station Manager Art McCraken was allowed a remote station set-up in the nearby Twelve Dozen Shop courtesy of the business owner, Mrs. John Gross." Eugene Grace even arranged for sports broadcasting legend Bill Stern to call the action over NBC radio. Stern would broadcast live from the golf course to a national audience. The added touch of including Stern was not without its challenges. "They had Bill Stern on a jeep, he could be 100 yards away, and you could still hear him," Billy explained. This proved to be a bit of a distraction as Billy recalls, "I missed three short putts in the final because of that."

According to Billy Maxwell, the turning point in the final match occurred during the morning round on the 203 yard 14th hole. All square coming off the 13th, Billy was first to tee off on the uphill par-3. He hit a 2-iron long and left into a triangular shaped bunker. Gagliardi answered by striking a beautiful 4-wood to within 10 feet.

Making his way into the bunker Billy carefully surveyed the situation. He had short-sided himself with the ball a mere 30 feet from the hole. The sand was wet and heavy, making a clean extrication much more difficult. After taking his stance, he took a deep breath and exhaled just before drawing back the open-faced club with the thumb and fore finger of his right hand. Picking the club up abruptly on the backswing, Billy gently transitioned to the downswing, accelerating the club so it would slide gently under and through the ball. On impact, he instinctively knew from the feel it was a good shot, but how good was anybody's guess. The green was running away from him, and his only reference would be the reaction from the large gallery encircling the green.

As the ball disappeared over the lip of the deep faced bunker, a brief moment of silence was broken by the rising murmur of the gallery as they watched the ball make its way down the slippery slope. As the ball rolled gently toward the vicinity of its intended target, it made one final detour 18 inches from the hole, breaking slightly to the right, placing it in direct line with the flagstick. The roar of several thousand voices signaled his ball had found the bottom of the hole. Billy made his way out of the bunker where the scene was pure pandemonium. It took two minutes for calm to be restored before Joe Gagliardi could attempt his putt.

With a wry smile, Billy explained, "I made it from the bunker, and he missed his birdie putt. Everything went my way after that."

Billy maintained his morning round momentum with impressive sand saves at 15 and 17. When asked about his remarkable play from the bunkers, Billy responded, "Those traps were just right...they were firm...reminded me of Texas sand." Billy was also employing a new piece of equipment during the U.S. Amateur. "I had a new sand wedge in my bag that week," Billy said. "I bought it out of a barrel in a Dallas pro shop. It was a Patty Berg model sand wedge," he explained.

When the afternoon round got under way, the exhausting effect of playing over 200 holes of golf during the previous seven days started to show on the near 40 year-old legs of Joe Gagliardi. The father of five pushed his opening tee shot on the par-5 first hole into the right fairway bunker. His second shot travelled even farther right into the trees resulting in a bogey six. On the second hole Joe regained control of his driver, only to three-putt for another bogey. Gagliardi was two over par the first four holes in the afternoon.

Contrary to his opponent's listless start, Maxwell seemed energized as the afternoon round began. During that same stretch, the younger Maxwell went on a birdie spree and won three of the first four holes to forge a seemingly insurmountable 5 up lead. Apparently Judge Gagliardi didn't receive the memo. The consummate competitor, Gagliardi courageously clawed his way back. His birdie on the 187 yard par 3, 11th reduced the margin to three holes, but that was all he could muster against an opponent whose game seemed to get stronger as the day wore on. Billy Maxwell would par the next four holes to register a 4 and 3 victory, and in doing so, become the first champion from the state of Texas, and at 22 years 2 months of age, the second youngest U.S. Amateur champion. Robert Gardner was 19 years 5 months old when he won his first of two amateur titles in 1909. Billy was 4 months younger than Bobby Jones when Jones won the championship in 1924 at Merion.

Billy became just the third college student to win in the 51 year history of the U.S. Amateur. Bob Gardner and Jess Sweetser were both students at Yale when they won their championships.

"I think I must be in a dream," Billy said. Surrounded by a large group of golf writers, casually sipping on a soft drink, young Billy now turned his attention toward other matters---"Classes begin on the 19th, and my wife is expecting to hear from me," he told the press.

CHAPTER THIRTEEN

The Fun is Over

"Friendships born on the field of athletic strife are the real gold of competition. Awards become corroded, friends gather no dust."

Jesse Owens

Over one thousand people, including the hundred plus members of the media, remained for the awards ceremony. The ceremony took place under the shade of several large Elm trees lining the pool area. Those present were treated to comments by Mr. Grace, USGA President James Standish, semifinalist Tommy Jacobs, runner-up Joe Gagliardi, and champion Billy Maxwell.

Mr. Standish congratulated both Saucon Valley Country Club and the city of Bethlehem. He called it "the finest tournament ever produced." Standish continued with his high praise:

> *"The standards of hospitality and tournament management were set so high by Saucon Valley that*

> *it is going to be very difficult for clubs in the future to equal them. Moreover, the examples in lack of commercialism and in real amateur spirit will long live in the memories of all your guests."*

From the organization of transportation, to the high quality food, and service in the clubhouse, no detail was overlooked. Course Superintendent Leonard Strong, Manager Daniel White, and Head Professional Ralph Hutchinson were all singled out for their contributions.

One of the most eloquent speeches came from runner-up Gagliardi. Joe "praised the production to the skies," saying:

> *"You made all the contestants happy with the kind and courteous treatment which was accorded to each and every one of us, and it is, I am sure, a memory which we will cherish the rest of our lives."*

Revealing a keen sense of humor, Gagliardi immediately switched gears and closed his remarks with the clever quip, "Only one thing was missing. Mr. Grace forgot to supply the boys with spending money!" Joe Gagliardi proved not only sharp on the links, but with the spoken word as well. The Giant Killer of Winged Foot would continue to excel on the golf course in the years to come but would be best remembered for his service as a longtime justice and administrative judge for the Ninth Judicial District of the State Supreme Court of New York. His most noted case came as a State Supreme Court Justice in 1964, when he presided over the child custody battle between Gov. Nelson A. Rockefeller's wife, Happy, and her former husband, Dr. James S. Murphy.

With the proceedings coming to a close, Mr. Grace announced, "The fun is over, we will tell Charley Wilson (Bethlehem Steel Plant Manager) that next week we go back to making steel!"

Where does Billy Maxwell rank his victory in the U.S. Amateur at Saucon Valley?

"It was the number one thing I ever did in my life!" he says. "Frank Stranahan said to me, I have a room full of trophies, but I'd give every one of those for the one you've got."

"It really opened some doors," Billy said. "Still today, it has been nearly 70 years and people come around and ask about it."

One door that almost didn't open, however, was immediately following the awards ceremony. Billy explains, "I remember one of the guys I was with wanted to have a beer after the awards ceremony. They wouldn't allow me in the clubhouse without a jacket. So he lent me a coat." The only problem was the owner of the jacket stood over 6 feet tall. Billy goes on to say, "...This coat was about a foot too long. That thing went all the way down to my knees," but it did get him through the door.

CHAPTER FOURTEEN

The Friendly Skies

"Keep close count of your nickels and dimes, stay away from whiskey, and never concede a putt."

Sam Snead

When it was time to leave town Billy was offered a ride on a private airplane. He explains, "There was this guy from down in Texas...when I finished playing he stayed around and watched my matches. That next morning I flew home with him, but he said 'I'll take you as far as Memphis, and then you can catch a flight to Dallas.' When we got on the plane he then tells me 'I've got to stop in Pittsburgh first.'" What happened next would be comical, if not for the fact it was absolutely frightening. Billy's pilot, using outdated charts, chose to land on an airfield that no longer existed! Billy continues, "In Pittsburgh we landed in a field. On the landing we were just going like crazy with all this stuff going past the plane. Cutting through all this stuff that had grown up on the old air field that hadn't been used for years! There wasn't any asphalt at all. We just landed on that dirt!"

Eventually Billy's "ride" dropped him off at the Memphis airport. After landing in Memphis, and with his golf clubs slung over his shoulder, he walked to the airline office to buy a ticket on a commercial flight to Dallas. Billy said with a smile, "I was still so elated it didn't feel like my feet ever hit the ground anyway." Only married six months, he was eager to return home to present his bride with the winner's medal.

Billy's wife ended up with the gold medal, but what about the Havemeyer Trophy? Billy goes on to explain, "Back in those days in order to play in a USGA tournament you had to represent a private club." One exception to this rule was the current U.S. Public Links Champion would receive an exemption into the U.S. Amateur. This is how Tommy Jacobs' cross-town rival, 20 year-old David Stanley, gained entry into the Amateur at Saucon Valley. Billy continues, "My good friend Shorty Hornbuckle was the Head Professional at the Odessa Country Club in Texas. Shorty allowed me to represent the club, and that's how I was able to play in the Amateur at Saucon Valley. The U.S. Amateur trophy was shipped to the Odessa Country Club to be displayed for one year."

On Friday morning, September 21, 1951, "The King of national amateur golf," and his bride arrived at the Midland-Odessa airport and received a royal reception from over 20 city officials, and friends. Surprised by the large crowd, M.K. exclaimed, "What is everybody doing here?" Mayor C.W. McCollum stepped forward to declare Saturday as "Billy Maxwell Day" in Odessa, Texas. Billy was awarded with a gold key to the city, while M. K. received a bouquet of yellow roses from Mrs. Catherine Gist, president of the Odessa Women's Golf Association.

When asked how he felt about his new national title, Billy, breaking out in a wide grin said, "I'm a mighty happy guy."

The Maxwell's would need to fly back to Dallas on Sunday since school began in Denton on Monday, but not before they participated in a whirlwind of events planned for the weekend. The agenda for their weekend stay in Odessa appeared in an article entitled "King Comes Home," appearing in the September 21, 1951 edition of The Odessa American:

> *"Friday --- 12:30, Mrs. Maxwell attends luncheon of Odessa Women's Golf Association, Billy Maxwell attends Rotary club; 6:15 –Billy guest on 15-minute radio program at KOSA; 7:50 – Introduction at Broncho Stadium, prior to football game."*

> *"Saturday --- Noon, Informal luncheon at country club; 2:00 p.m. – 18 hole golf match with Maxwell and Bill Oliver or Shorty Hornbuckle playing Dode Forrester, Hobbs, N.M. and Bob French; 7:00 p.m. – barbecue at club served by Odessa Chuck Wagon Gang; 8:00 p.m. – testimonial ceremony at club and presentation of National Amateur trophy to club president Balie Griffith."*

> *"The golf match and barbecue Saturday is open to the public at $2.50 per person."*

In addition to all the accolades, Billy's victory in the U.S. Amateur Championship created many new opportunities. An invitation to play in the British Amateur was one. He remembers the 1952 Amateur Championship held at the Prestwick Golf Club in Scotland. On this particular occasion he caught a ride with Eddie Lowery, Harvie Ward, and a few others on an airplane chartered by Lowery. Lowery was a very successful automobile dealer in the San Francisco Bay area. Eddie Lowery was most famous, however, as a result of his first career---as Francis Ouimet's 10 year-old caddy in the 1913 U.S. Open Championship.

Ouimet won in a playoff against the two giants of the game, Harry Vardon and Ted Ray. In between golf tournaments Harvie Ward's day job was a salesman at Van-Etta Motors, Lowery's Lincoln-Mercury dealership in San Francisco; and after all he was very successful at it, having learned the trade from the master. Whenever West Coast Eddie spoke his Boston accent would always betray him. On more than one occasion Lowery was overheard talking on the telephone from a golf course saying "I'm gonna sell you a cah!"

Billy played well at Prestwick, making it to the round of 16. After the British Amateur, the group travelled to Paris to compete in the French Amateur at the Mortefontaine Club. Billy made it all the way to the finals against *Time Magazine's* "Ben Hogan of Amateur Golf," Dick Chapman. Billy led one up after the morning round. In the afternoon his usually accurate tee ball suddenly developed an interest in tall fescue, and Chapman rallied for the 4 and 3 win and his second French Amateur title.

Billy's adventure in the friendly skies part II occurred when their plane suffered a flat tire on landing. As Billy describes it, "We landed in Goose Bay (Labrador). The plane had a flat tire so they had to call New York for a new tire...we had to wait there for the tire." Billy remembers it being so cold no one could go outside. It was Billy's one and only trip to play competitive golf in Europe. Even later as a professional he never played in the British Open. It didn't make economic sense to make the trip. As he explained it, "There wasn't much money to be won in those days."

CHAPTER FIFTEEN

Dynamite

"I've always believed that there are funny people everywhere, but they're not just comedians. In fact, some of my best comedic inspirations were not professional entertainers."

Steve Martin

Another benefit of winning the U.S. Amateur is an invitation to play in the Masters Tournament in Augusta, Georgia. In 1952 Billy would play in his first, and only, Masters as an amateur. He would go on to play eleven more times but as a professional.

Whenever you find yourself in new surroundings, it's always nice to see a familiar face. On Billy's first trip to Augusta that face belonged to fellow amateur William Goodloe Jr. Billy first met Goodloe at the 1950 U.S. Amateur in Minneapolis and they became good friends. Goodloe was a short, stocky, ex-football player from Valdosta, Georgia. He possessed a very dynamic and charismatic personality, hence his nickname "Dynamite." Goodloe's penchant for attracting attention followed him everywhere he went. In the August 19, 1951 edition of _The Boston Post_, Gerry Moore previews the U.S. Amateur Championship, and describes the many amenities available at Saucon Valley Country Club. When Moore mentions the club's beautiful swimming pool Goodloe finds his way into the story:

> *"There is even a swimming pool in which the colorful Dynamite Goodloe of Valdosta, Georgia, can strut his diving stuff as he did two years ago at Oak Hill in Rochester, N.Y., and almost diverted all attention from the golf championship!"*

Dynamite Goodloe, a Walker Cup alternate in 1949, had an outstanding golf game to go along with his colorful personality. Dynamite Goodloe's two biggest fans were no other than Masters co-founders Clifford Roberts and Bobby Jones. "Cliff Roberts and Bobby Jones really loved this guy," Billy said.

The year before, at the 1951 Masters, Dynamite found himself five shots off Ben Hogan's lead going into the final round. In those days the leaders were not necessarily paired together in the final round. This practice didn't change until years' later as golf tournaments began to be televised. "Bobby Jones would always pair Dynamite with Byron Nelson. They really liked Byron," Billy explained. The favorable pairing didn't seem to provide any advantage on this particular occasion, however, as Dynamite exploded all the way to an 88!

At the '52 Masters, as the boys prepared to tee off for a practice round, they were approached by Clifford Roberts. "Cliff Roberts asked if we would like to meet the Duke of Windsor, and we said, yeah, oh yeah," Billy explained. Roberts goes on to say, "Okay, I'll send a driver out to the course with a cart, and we'll bring y'all in." Billy continues, "So we're out on the

15th hole, and they came out and got us. They took us up to Bobby Jones' cottage... so we go in, and Dynamite said we should introduce Billy first because he's our champion. Now everything Dynamite did was Mister, it was always Mister. So I shook hands with the Duke of Windsor. He was a little guy, and very well dressed." Then Cliff Roberts says, "Here we have this fellow, and Dynamite Goodloe is his name," and the Duke responds, "Well that's just fine." Roberts continues with the introduction, "Please meet His Royal Highness Edward, Duke of Windsor." At that point Dynamite Goodloe rushes forward to vigorously shake the hand of the former King of England, exclaiming, "Mister Duke, I've been wanting to meet you all my life!" "Dynamite was such a comical guy," Billy said, "Everybody liked him."

It should be noted that Dynamite Goodloe was very consistent when it came to meeting royalty. A few years later when introduced to Prince Charles he reportedly addressed the heir to the British throne as "Mister Prince."

Dynamite Goodloe would later become the long-time Coach of the Georgia Tech freshman football team, and would be Georgia Tech Coach Bobby Dodd's top recruiter. In 1985 William "Dynamite" Goodloe Jr. was inducted into the Georgia Sports Hall of Fame. In 1989, he would join his good friend Bobby Jones as an inaugural member of the Georgia Golf Hall of Fame. Clifford Roberts would follow them into the Hall of Fame in 1992.

CHAPTER SIXTEEN

South of the Border

"Don't play too much golf. Two rounds a day are plenty."

Harry Vardon

A very popular tournament in the 1950's, especially for the players from Texas, was the Mexican Amateur. Billy played in several of Mexico's national championships over the years, including the Mexican Open. He won the championship as a professional in 1956 with a record score of 264, which still stands today.

The 1953 Mexican Amateur was one of Billy's final tournaments as an amateur. He faced familiar adversary Frank Stranahan of Toledo, Ohio, in the finals. As Billy tells it, "I played Frank Stranahan in the Mexican Amateur once before (1951) and he beat me. The next time we played against each other in Mexico (1953) I thought for sure he was going to beat me again." Billy goes on, "This time was my time though. I had him six down after 17 holes in the morning round. He came running up to me on the 17th fairway saying 'Nobody ever shot this kind of golf against me.'" After going 10 up at the 24th hole, Billy remembers saying, "Why don't we just play the next four holes because that would bring us close to the clubhouse? Don't you know after I said that, he birdied four holes in a row!" It was too little too late for The Toledo Strongman. Stranahan was 4-under par through 29 holes, but lost to Billy, who was an incredible 12-under par for the match. "It was the best golf I ever played in my life," Billy said. The next morning's headline in The New York Times said it all, "Maxwell vanquishes Stranahan 8 and 7 to Capture Mexican Amateur Golf Title."

Stranahan's devotion to physical fitness and proper nutrition was certainly an anomaly in the 1950's. If Billy was playing that much better, and if a special diet was responsible, Stranahan wanted to know the secret! During the afternoon round, after watching Billy drain yet another birdie, Stranahan couldn't contain himself any longer. He came right up to Billy and asked, "What do you eat?" As the old saying goes, Frankie was "in the right church, but the wrong pew." As it turned out it wasn't what Billy Maxwell ate, but rather what he *didn't* eat that made the difference. "I never ate before an afternoon match," Billy said, "Even at Saucon Valley I never ate between rounds."

By holding to his erstwhile eating habits, Billy was able to maintain his energy, and focus, while his opponents typically struggled later in the day. During the Amateur at Saucon Valley most contestants couldn't resist the magnificent food placed before them by the Saucon Valley staff. Billy, on the other hand, would pass the time on the front steps of the clubhouse in quiet reflection or engage in an occasional chat with Club Manager Daniel White.

Billy was right about all the great players from Texas---they're just a little more hungry.

CHAPTER SEVENTEEN

Draft Day

"If you watch a game, it's fun. If you play at it, it's recreation. If you work at it, it's golf."

Bob Hope

It was on one of the trips south of the border where Billy and his North Texas State teammates ran afoul of Joe Dey and the USGA. Evidently there was concern with regard to expenses covered for the boys while in Mexico. The ruling body revoked the amateur status of all involved. "The USGA made all of us from North Texas pros after we played in a tournament in Mexico," Billy said. His dream of playing on the 1953 Walker Cup Team was now just a distant memory.

As it turned out, it didn't make any difference, because shortly thereafter Billy received his draft notice for induction into the armed services. He served nearly two years in the U.S. Army stationed at Ft. Hood, Texas. By coincidence, the pro at Ft. Hood was retiring, so Billy fit nicely into his new surroundings. Billy explained, "The pro was retiring...so they made me the pro at the Ft. Hood Golf Course." Ironically, the USGA reinstated his amateur status while he was still serving in the Army. That didn't matter though, because immediately following his discharge, Private First Class and Mrs. Maxwell jumped in the car and headed for the Southern California Open and their new life together on the PGA Tour.

In the early 1950's the PGA Tour season began at Los Angeles, would then move next to Palm Springs, and from there everyone would travel up the coast to the Crosby Clambake at Pebble Beach. In those days the Maxwell's travelled between tour stops towing a Gulfstream trailer. Equipped with the necessary amenities, the trailer provided all the comforts of home. On one of these occasions between tour stops in Los Angeles, the Maxwell's only child, Melanie, would be welcomed into the world.

At each stop along the way, the Hollywood elite would lend their star power for the pre-tournament Pro Am. "Those movie stars really helped the PGA Tour back then," Billy said. "The fans would come to see them, and then they'd see what kind of players we had...it was always a fun time."

Billy became acquainted with both Bing Crosby and Bob Hope. "Crosby was a real man's man," Billy remembers. The golf celebrity triumvirate on the west coast in those days was Crosby, Hope, and Bob Goldwater. "Bob Hope and Bing Crosby really liked him," Billy said. Goldwater, in addition to being the driving force behind the Phoenix Open, was an excellent amateur player. "I first met Bob in 1950 at the Dallas Country Club. He was runner-up to Charlie Coe in the Western Amateur," Billy said. Goldwater was also an Arizona Amateur Champion, and had earned low amateur honors in the Arizona Open as well. Billy goes on, "He was my best buddy! Bob came to me once and said, 'I got a guy who's going to be the next great player. He's a left-hander.'"

Bob Goldwater proved to have excellent instincts as a talent scout. Bob Charles of New Zealand would go on to win over 70 professional tournaments worldwide, and become the first left-handed golfer to win a major championship (1963 British Open). Sir Robert James Charles was inducted into the World Golf Hall of Fame in 2008.

Billy came very close to winning his buddy's tournament on two occasions. In both 1955 and 1969, Billy finished tied for second in the Phoenix Open behind winner Gene Littler. In 1955, Billy and a young Arnold Palmer both finished one stroke behind at 276. It was that year when Maxwell, Palmer, and Littler all played early the final day, and managed to finish just before a massive dust storm engulfed the course. Third round leader Jay Herbert wasn't so fortunate. He started late, and played most of the final round in unimaginable conditions. Herbert's five shot lead blew away along with everything else that wasn't nailed down that day at the Arizona Country Club.

In 1969 there were no storms and the scoring conditions were perfect. Billy, Don January, and Miller Barber all finished at 19 under par, but fell two strokes shy of Littler's amazing 21 under par score of 263. Phoenix business owner, Wade Borg, was Billy's 15 year-old caddy in the 1969 Phoenix Open. Although just a youngster, Wade was no rookie. The previous summer he defeated the medalist, an older more experienced player, in the opening round of the Arizona Junior Championship. Wade's father, Emil, was a member of the Arizona Country Club, and Wade learned the game growing up at the club. He also knew the greens like the back of his hand. "The first hole of the tournament Billy asked me how his putt would break," Wade recalls. "He made that putt and from then on took my advice on every putt. It was unusual since I was only 15 years old, but he made every putt from 10 feet the rest of the way."

Many years later while attending a Champion's Tour event at Hillcrest Country Club in Sun City, Arizona, Wade spotted Billy on the practice range. "I stopped to say hello," Wade said. "I didn't expect him to remember me, but he did."

It's impossible to forget a great caddy.

CHAPTER EIGHTEEN

Ryder Cup

"The most important shot in golf is the next one."

Ben Hogan

Billy played some of the best golf of his career in the early 1960's. During the '62 and '63 seasons he had top 5 finishes in the three major championships he entered (Masters, U.S. Open, and PGA Championship). Billy also won the 1962 Dallas Open Invitational (Bryon Nelson Classic) with a score of 277, four shots ahead of runner-up Johnny Pott. Billy recalls, "I never did have a big payday." He continues, "The Azalea Open in Wilmington, North Carolina, was my first PGA Tour win. I won $2,800. The Dallas Open in 1962 I made $5,300 for the win. Now it's just unbelievable. They'd think you were crazy if you mentioned back then they would someday play for a million dollars in a tournament!"

A victory at the 1961 Palm Springs (Bob Hope) Classic marked Billy's fifth win on the PGA Tour. He collected just over $5,000 for his efforts, but it was college teammate Don

January's 40th place finish in the same event he remembers most. There was a hole-in-one contest conducted during the tournament, with $50,000 up for grabs. January earned $18.34 for five rounds of tournament play, but padded his wallet by jarring his ball for the hole-in-one and the $50,000 prize. That single shot was worth only $14,000 less than what Gary Player eventually won as the Tour's leading money leader that season.

"He never let me forget that," Billy said with a chuckle.

Billy started off his best PGA Tour season with the 22 under-par victory. Later he won the Insurance City Open (beating Ted Kroll in seven playoff holes) and finished the year a career-best 10th place on the money list—with $28,335. His great play earned him the right to represent the United States in the 1963 Ryder Cup to be held at the Atlanta Athletic Club, at the site now known as the East Lake Golf Club in Atlanta, Georgia.

The U.S. team was led by playing captain Arnold Palmer. 1963 would mark the last year anyone served as a playing captain for either side. The main story line that year, however, involved Palmer's young rival, Jack Nicklaus. Despite having won his third major title at the PGA Championship earlier that summer, Nicklaus was ineligible to play due to rules set in place by the PGA of America. Nicklaus would eventually gain membership into the PGA and would begin representing his country in the Ryder Cup in 1969. Eligibility rules have since changed, allowing talented young players to earn a spot on the team through a points system. Current rules also allow for two "captain's picks" as well. It was Nicklaus who suggested changing the format of the matches to include players from continental Europe on the Great Britain side. This was done in an effort to make the matches more competitive, as the U.S. team usually won by a lopsided margin. Beginning in 1979 the inclusion of great players like Seve Ballesteros of

Spain and Bernhard Langer of Germany set the stage for more competitive Ryder Cups in the future.

Billy Maxwell played superb golf throughout the entire Ryder Cup. Employing the same technique used at Saucon Valley, Billy would apply pressure on his opponents by placing his approach shots closer to the hole. Even on the longer holes at East Lake, Billy consistently hit his 4-wood inside the iron shots of his longer hitting opponents.

In Foursomes competition he teamed up with Bob Goalby to defeat Dave Thomas and Harry Weetman by the margin of 4 and 3. Billy remembers the special pressure felt in the Ryder Cup and how it affected teammate Goalby. "I was standing next to Bob Goalby during opening ceremonies...He elbowed me in the ribs and said, 'I don't think I can tee off, how 'bout you?' I looked over and thought he was going to get sick." Billy goes on to explain, "So I told him I would hit it."

In Four-Ball matches he and Billy Casper joined forces twice, and won both matches. In Singles Billy played his best golf defeating the great Christy O'Connor by a margin of 2 and 1. The U.S. squad won by the resounding score of 23 to 9. Billy Maxwell completed his one and only Ryder Cup appearance with a perfect 4-0-0 record.

One reason for Billy's superb play was his trusted friend Patty Berg -- his Patty Berg sand wedge, that is. The same club he used to hole out against Joe Gagliardi in the U.S. Amateur was in the bag for the Ryder Cup. "I used that same club for the next twenty years, including 15 years on the PGA Tour," Billy said. He would continue to use this same sand wedge "until the Wilson Company insisted I play with a newer model." Billy goes on to explain the differences between today's technology and the tools of the trade back in the day. "Back then you didn't have all these lofts available. You used this same club for all type of shots. If you needed more loft you just opened up the face. Eddie Lowery was actually in the habit of opening up a 9 iron to use out of bunkers."

What advice would the holder of a perfect Ryder Cup record offer to today's players?

"They just need to think better," Billy said. He goes on to say, "It's like Tommy Bolt once said, "These guys are getting so good they aren't eating enough hamburgers and hot dogs."

With regard to Arnold Palmer's leadership as a team captain, Billy said, "Everything Arnold Palmer did was good. We liked everything he did. He'd say, 'would you like to play with this other fellow today?' You'd say yes or no. He would always ask you. He was King, but everybody liked him. He would say the right thing at the right time. He didn't throw his club when he missed a shot. Everybody liked Arnold in the locker room, and all around."

When asked if Palmer was considered a fierce competitor, Billy's response was emphatic, "You said it right there! But he is definitely a good guy."

Was there anyone else on tour in those days with exceptional talent, but perhaps didn't go down in history with as much recognition? Billy didn't hesitate, "Doug Ford was always good! He was a winner. He won more tournaments in one ten year period on the tour than anyone, and a nicer guy never came down the pike. He never said much. He just let his clubs do the talking."

The 19th Hole
Jacksonville

"But in the end it's still a game of golf, and if at the end of the day you can't shake hands with your opponents and still be friends, then you've missed the point."

Payne Stewart

Throughout his professional career Billy Maxwell made 443 starts on the PGA Tour, including 12 appearances in the Masters. Along with seven career victories he had three top ten finishes in the U.S. Open, and Masters, with two top tens' in the PGA Championship. Billy's best major championship finish was a tie for fifth in each of the majors played on American soil. Billy Maxwell's stellar career was highlighted in 1982 with his induction into the Texas Golf Hall of Fame.

The golf course Billy grew up on in Abilene, Texas, is still there, although under a new name---Maxwell Municipal Golf Course. Billy shares, "Everybody thinks it was named after me, but it's named after my father. Before he died the city government bought it and renamed it Maxwell Municipal."

These days Billy hangs his hat at the Hyde Park Golf Club in Jacksonville, Florida. Billy and former PGA Tour player Chris Blocker purchased the course in 1971. Designed by famed architect Donald Ross, Hyde Park was a regular stop on both the men's and women's professional tours in the 1940's and 1950's. The Hyde Park tournament preceded both the Jacksonville Open and The Player's Championship. All the greats of the game played at Hyde Park, including Mickey Wright, who won her first professional event there in 1956. It was during the 1947 Jacksonville Open, when Ben Hogan had a less than memorable experience at Hyde Park. Billy explains, "He (Hogan) was asked what was the highest score he ever made on a hole, and he said 'I remember that like it was yesterday. It was Hyde Park in Jacksonville. I made eleven on a par three hole.'" The par three sixth hole is a relatively short 151 yards, but is guarded on the entire right side by a particularly large deep faced bunker. Aiming left to avoid the bunker, Hogan missed the green hitting his ball into the water hazard. Without the benefit of a designated drop area, Hogan tried the same shot over and over again. Unfortunately, his ball rolled down the slope and into the small pond several times. Adding insult to injury, Hogan was leading the tournament at the time.

Today, 86 years young, Billy Maxwell either plays golf or practices at least 5 days a week. Billy has moved into the 21st century in style, arriving for his golf dates at TPC Sawgrass via Uber. He's shot his age so many times over the years the family has lost count, although it's been nearly a year since he last accomplished the feat. When he's not playing he enjoys watching today's PGA Tour professionals on television, and marvels at the distance modern players drive the ball. When there's no live golf on TV, he watches instructional videos of his childhood hero, Bobby Jones. His greatest enjoyment, however, comes from watching his grandson, Garrett Bevill, a promising young professional, "hit that ball a mile."

It's a long walk from the dusty roads of a small Texas town to the lush fairways of the PGA Tour, but Billy Maxwell made the trip, and he did it with style and grace. Along the way he won the most important tournament of his life, and although he's made a living playing golf, he has never forgotten the real reason he plays is simply for the love of the game.

—

Bibliography and Notes

Chapter 1 – Abilene

Billy Maxwell – meeting/interview, TPC Sawgrass Champion's Locker Room, April 21, 2015.

Melanie Bevill – meeting/interview, TPC Sawgrass Champion's Locker Room, April 21, 2015, and subsequent telephone and email correspondence in June and July, 2015.

Golfworld Magazine, September 21, 1951.

Wikipedia, Billy Maxwell.

Wikipedia, Don January.

Golfworld Magazine, May 5, 1948.

Dallas News, August 11, 1948.

Chapter 2 – Legends of Texas Golf

Billy Maxwell – meeting/interview, TPC Sawgrass Champion's Locker Room, April 21, 2015.

Hogan, Curt Sampson, 1997, Three Rivers Press.

Trenham Golf History, *The Leaders and Legends 1940 to 1949*, Pete Trenham, PGA

Wikipedia, Jimmy Demaret.

Chapter 3 – Spirit of the Game

The Boys Life of Bobby Jones, O.B. Keeler, 1931, Harper & Brothers, Sleeping Bear Press.

The Bobby Jones Story, O.B. Keeler, 2003, Triumph Books.

Official Program 51st United States Amateur Championship, September 10-15, 1951, Saucon Valley Country Club.

Wikipedia, Eugene G. Grace.

Lehigh Valley Golf Hall of Fame, induction class of 2015, biography of Eugene Grace.

Country Club Topics, Saucon Valley Country Club-Final Tournament Report, December 1951.

Wikipedia, Herbert Strong.

Wikipedia, Francis Ouimet.

Wikipedia, List of Ticker Tape Parades in New York City.

Lehigh University Archives, Biography of Eugene Grace.

Ancestry.com, John Wesley Grace.

Brian McCall, lunch/meeting, Saucon Valley Country Club Locker Lounge, September 1, 2012.

A Centennial Tribute to Golf in Philadelphia, James W. Finnegan, 1996, The Golf Association of Philadelphia.

Allentown Morning Call, *Playing of National Amateur at Saucon Tribute to Effort of Golfer Eugene Grace*, by Bud Weiser, September 9, 1951.

The New York Times, *Chapman Heads New Metropolitan Golf Association Handicap Rating at Plus 1*, September 9, 1951.

USGA at 120, Part 1: America's Early Golf Heroes, USGA video library.

Allentown Morning Call, *Don't Miss This One! Philadelphia Eagles vs. N.Y. Giants*, September 13, 1951.

Chapter 4 – The Big Dance

USGA, 1951 U.S. Amateur Championship file, USGA Library.

Clyde Oskin, Jr. – telephone interview, May 21, 2015.

Bethlehem Globe-Times, Longest Hole Ever Played in the Amateur, by Oscar Fraley, August 23, 1951.

Debbie Moore, meeting/interview, Saucon Valley Country Club Administration office, September 14, 2015.

Golfworld Magazine, September 7, 1951.

Golfworld Magazine, September 21, 1951.

Lifelong Looper, The Story of a Caddie Legend, by Cindy O'Krepki, 2005, Bluestreak Publishing, LLC.

The Morning Call, Saucon: A Course You Don't Forget, by John Kunda, September 24, 1987.

Report of Activities of Program and Publicity Committee, 51st U.S. Amateur Championship, Saucon Valley Country Club archives.

Billy Maxwell, meeting/interview, TPC Sawgrass Champion's Locker Room, April 21, 2015.

Jim White, lunch meeting/interview, Saucon Valley Country Club Locker Lounge, May 28, 2015.

Tom McHale, lunch meeting/interview, Saucon Valley Country Club Locker Lounge, June 25, 2015.

James Roney, meeting/interview, Saucon Valley Country Club, Golf Superintendent office, June 22, 2015.

Chapter 5 – Love at First Sight

USGA, 1951 U.S. Amateur Championship file, USGA Library.

Golfworld Magazine, September 21, 1951.

Bethlehem Globe-Times, Sports, September 10, 1951.

USGA News Release, August 22, 1951.

Allentown Morning Call, *Three Golfing Careys,* September 10, 1951.

Golfworld Magazine, *Qualifiers By Sections,* September 7, 1951.

Saucon Valley Country Club, Club archives, 1951 U.S. Amateur, Vol. 1-5.

Golf Association of Philadelphia Magazine, *2012 Hall of Fame Howard Everitt,* Fall, 2012.

Kellygolfhistory.com, Howard Everitt and Stan Dudas.

Doc Giffin, email correspondence from Arnold Palmer, July 20, 2015.

David Derminio, electronic communication, July 29, 2015.

Chapter 6 – Guess Who's Coming to Dinner

USGA, 1951 U.S. Amateur Championship file, USGA Library.

Allentown Evening Chronicle, *Urzetta Sets Good Example,* by Oscar Fraley, September 11, 1951.

Chapter 7 – Who's Who

The New York Times, Sports, September 14, 1951.

Billy Maxwell, meeting/interview, TPC Sawgrass Champion's Locker Room, April 21, 2015.

Golfworld Magazine, September 21, 1951.

Golfworld Magazine, September 7, 1951.

Bethlehem Globe-Times, Sports, September 10, 1951.

Philly.com, *James B. McHale, Jr., 81, Golf Pro,* June 18, 1997.

The New York Times, *Cards of the Leaders, Third Round, Final Round,* June 14, 1947.

A Centnnial Tribute to Golf in Philadelphia, by James W. Finnegan, 1996, The Golf Association of Philadelphia.

Martin Emeno, Golf Association of Philadelphia, several telephone and email communications regarding James B. McHale, Jr., July 2015.

Tom McHale, lunch/meeting interview, Saucon Valley Country Club Locker Lounge, June 25, 2015, and subsequent telephone conversations, June and July 2015.

San Bernadino County Sun, *New York Pro Cuts 12 Strokes Off Par With Brilliant 276*, January 6, 1936.

Wikipedia, The Walker Cup.

Hilary Cronheim, USGA Special Collections Librarian, several email communications, July 2015.

Victoria Student, USGA Junior Historian, email correspondence, July 28, 2015.

A Game of Golf: A Book of Reminiscence, by Francis Ouimet, 1978, Old Golf Shop, Inc.

USGA.ORG, Past Presidents, USGA.

Wikipedia, Carol Semple Thompson.

Wikipedia, John S. Battle

David Staebler, USGA, Director of Rules Education, several email and telephone communications, July and August, 2015.

Pennsylvania Golf Association, Championship History.

Saucon Valley Country Club, Club archives, 1951 U.S. Amateur, Vol. 1-5.

Bethlehem Globe-Times, *McHale In Action At Saucon Valley*, June 9, 1951.

Allentown Morning Call, *U.S. Walker Cup Golfers Top Canadians, 10 To 2,* by Bud Weiser, September 8, 1951.

Wikipedia, Robert Goldwater.

Wikipedia, Phoenix Open.

USGA, 1951 U.S. Amateur Championship file, USGA Library.

Allentown Morning Call, *Two Eagle Man,* September 12, 1951.

Michael Cumberpatch, Mid-Atlantic Golf Association, several email communications, June and July, 2015.

Jerry Hoesteter, Lancaster Country Club, several electronic communications, July 8, 2015.

The Bobby Jones Story, by O.B. Keeler, 2003, Triumph Books.

Allentown Morning Call, Sports, September 11, 1951.

Dallas Morning News, *As Ben Hogan's Closest Living Relative Jacque Hogan Towery has Memories of Late Champ That Don't Exist in History Books,* by Brad Townsend, May 25, 2013.

Chapter 8 – Rhapsody in Blue

Bethlehem Globe-Times, Sports, September 12, 1951.

Golfworld Magazine, September 21, 1951.

Billy Maxwell, meeting/interview, TPC Sawgrass Champion's Locker Room, April 21, 2015.

Chapter 9 – Kris Kringle Bounced in the Christmas City

The New York Times, Sports, September 9, 1951; September 11, 1951.

Allentown Morning Call, Sports, September 11, 1951.

Golfworld Magazine, September 21, 1951.

Rick McCall, telephone interview, August 12, 2015.

USGA, 1951 U.S. Amateur Championship file, USGA Library.

Bethlehem Globe-Times, Sports, September 11, 1951.

Chapter 10 – Stymie

Merriam-Webster Dictionary, *Stymie.*

Wikipedia, *Stymie.*

Golfweek Magazine, September 6, 2011.

Ruleshistory.com, *Stymie.*

The Golf Dictionary, *The Stymie*, by Michael Corcoran, 1997, Taylor Publishing

Application for Entry, Rules of Amateur Status, 1951 Amateur Championship of the United States Golf Association.

Wikipedia, Walter Hagen.

David Staebler, USGA, Director of Rules Education, lunch/meeting, Golf House, Far Hills, N.J., June 19, 2015, and several subsequent telephone and email communications, July, August, and September 2015.

Bernie Loehr, USGA, Director of Amateur Status (retired), telephone interview, September 3, 2015, and subsequent email communications.

Chapter 11 – The Seige Gun of South Hills Country Club

Bethlehem Globe-Times, Sports, September 11-14, 1951.

The New York Times, Sports, September 11-14, 1951.

Allentown Morning Call, Sports, September 11-14, 1951; September 24, 1987.

Golfworld Magazine, September 21, 1951.

John Benson (no relation), telephone interview, May 12, 2015.

USGA, 1950 U.S. Amateur Championship file, USGA Library.

USGA, 1951 U.S. Amateur Championship file, USGA Library.

USGA, 1952 U.S. Amateur Championship file, USGA Library.

Tomwatson.com.

Wikipedia, Bo Wininger.

Wikipedia, Tom Strange.

Wikipedia, Billy Maxwell.

Bill McGuiness, telephone interview, May 26, 2015.

PGATOUR.COM, tournament history.

Billy Maxwell, meeting/interview, TPC Sawgrass Champion's Locker Room, April 21, 2015.

A Game of Golf: A Book of Reminiscence, by Francis Ouimet, 1978, Old Golf Shop, Inc.

GSGA.ORG, Georgia Golf Hall of Fame, Arnold Blum, Robert T. Jones, Jr.

Saucon Valley Country Club, club archives, 1951 U.S. Amateur, Vol. 1-5.

Jim White, lunch meeting/interview, Saucon Valley Country Club Locker Lounge, May 28, 2015, and subsequent telephone and email communications.

Wikipedia, Henry Picard.

Bethlehem Globe-Times, *Sports Parade,* by Oscar Fraley, September 14, 1951.

Power Golf, by Ben Hogan, November 2, 2010, Gallery Books.

Masters.com, tournament records.

Chapter 12 – The West Texas Cyclone vs. Giant Killer of Winged Foot

Bethlehem Globe-Times, Sports, September 15-16, 1951.

Allentown Morning Call, Sports, September15-16, 1951.

The New York Times, Sports, September 15-16, 1951.

Reading Eagle, Sports, September 15, 1951.

Golfworld Magazine, September 21, 1951.

Saucon Valley Country Club, club archives, 1951 U.S. Amateur, Vol. 1-5.

Bethlehem Globe-Times, *Swing Along Athletic Row,* by Fred Nonnemacher, September 17, 1951.

Billy Maxwell, meeting/interview, TPC Sawgrass Champion's Locker Room, April 21, 2015.

Jim White, lunch meeting/interview, Saucon Valley Country Club Locker Lounge, May 28, 2015, and subsequent telephone and email communications.

Chapter 13 – The Fun is Over

Golfworld, Magazine, September 21, 1951.

The New York Times, Justice Gagliardi is bid Farewell, November 22, 1987.

The New York Times, Joseph F. Gagliardi, 80, longtime justice, May 4, 1992.

Billy Maxwell, meeting/interview, TPC Sawgrass Champion's Locker Room, April 21, 2015.

Jim White, lunch meeting/interview, Saucon Valley Country Club Locker Lounge, May 28, 2015, and subsequent telephone and email communications.

Saucon Valley Country Club, club archives, 1951 U.S. Amateur, Vol. 1-5.

Chapter 14 – The Friendly Skies

Billy Maxwell, meeting/interview, TPC Sawgrass Champion's Locker Room, April 21, *2015.*

Application for Entry, 1951 Amateur Championship of the United States Golf Association.

USGA, 1951 U.S. Amateur Championship file, USGA Library.

The New York Times, Chapman Rallies for Victory Over Maxwell, June 10, 1952.

Saucon Valley Country Club, club archives, 1951 U.S. Amateur, Vol. 1-5.

The Odessa American, King Comes Home, September 21, 1951.

The Match: The Day the Game of Golf Changed Forever, by Mark Frost, 2007, Hyperion.

Chapter 15 – Dynamite

GSGA.ORG, Georgia Golf Hall of Fame, William Goodloe, Jr.

Georgia Sports Hall of Fame, William Goodloe, Jr.

Wikipedia, Dynamite Goodloe.

The Boston Post, *U.S. Amateur Preview*, by Gerry Moore, August 19, 1951.

Official Program 51st United States Amateur Championship, September 10-15, 1951.

Billy Maxwell, meeting/interview, TPC Sawgrass Champion's Locker Room, April 21, 2015.

Masters.com, tournament history.

Chapter 16 – South of the Border

Billy Maxwell, meeting/interview, TPC Sawgrass Champion's Locker Room, April 21, 2015.

The New York Times, *Maxwell Vanquishes Stranahan, 8 and 7, To Capture Mexican Amateur Golf Title*, November 2, 1953.

Chapter 17 – Draft Day

Billy Maxwell, meeting/interview, TPC Sawgrass Champion's Locker Room, April 21, 2015.

The Florida Times-Union, *Thanks for the Memories: Jacksonville's Billy Maxwell won Bob Hope event 50 years ago*, by Garry Smits, January 20, 2011.

Azcentral.com, Past Champions Phoenix Open.

Wade Borg, telephone interview, June 27, 2015.

GOLFWGV.COM, World Golf Hall of Fame, Bob Charles.

Chapter 18 – Ryder Cup

Billy Maxwell, meeting/interview, TPC Sawgrass Champion's Locker Room, April 21, 2015.

RYDERCUP.COM, 1963 Ryder Cup.

<u>*Official Program 2016 Arnold Palmer Invitational*</u>, *Arnold Palmer – The Last Playing Captain*, by Williiam Godfrey.

<u>*The Florida Times-Union,*</u> *Thanks for the Memories: Jacksonville's Billy Maxwell won Bob Hope event 50 years ago,* by Garry Smits, January 20, 2011.

19th Hole – Jacksonville

Billy Maxwell, meeting/interview, TPC Sawgrass Champion's Locker Room, April 21,2015.

Hydeparkgolfclub.com, club history.

Melanie Bevill, meeting/interview, TPC Sawgrass Champion's Locker Room, April 21, 2015. Subsequent email and telephone correspondence, June and July, 2015.

Texas Golf Hall of Fame, Billy Maxwell class of 1982.

Photograph/Image Credits

Cover Photo – (Left to right) Joe Gagliardi, Eugene Grace, and Billy Maxwell on the first tee prior to the final match of the 1951 U.S. Amateur Championship.
(Photo courtesy of Saucon Valley Country Club)

Inside the book photos

The media center at Saucon Valley Country Club, referred to as "the most palatial press headquarters in golfing history," featured special lighting and custom-built individual typewriter stations.
(Photo courtesy of Saucon Valley Country Club)

Eugene Gifford Grace, Patriarch of Saucon Valley Country Club.
(Photo courtesy of Saucon Valley Country Club)

Leonard Strong, Course Superintendent. Strong was the younger brother of course architect Herbert Strong.
(Photo courtesy of Saucon Valley Country Club)

Billy Maxwell, a 22 year-old college student, became the second youngest U.S. Amateur champion and first champion from the state of Texas.

(Photo courtesy of Saucon Valley Country Club)

Charles "Chick" Evans (left), 1916 U.S. Open and U.S. Amateur champion, with Eugene Grace. The Amateur championship at Saucon Valley marked the 42nd consecutive appearance in the U.S. Amateur for Evans.

(Photo courtesy of Saucon Valley Country Club)

All the greats played in the U.S. Amateur at Saucon Valley. (From left to right) Robert Knowles, 1950 French Amateur champion; Sam Urzetta, 1950 U.S. Amateur champion; Richard Chapman, 1951 British Amateur champion.

(Photo courtesy of Saucon Valley Country Club)

Tommy Jacobs, 16, 1951 U.S. Junior Amateur champion (left), poses with good friend David Stanley, 20, 1951 U.S. Amateur Public Links champion. Both young men hailed from the same home town of Montebello, California.

(Photo courtesy of Saucon Valley Country Club)

Saucon Valley legend Ross "Cotton" Young caddied for Dale Morey in the 1951 U.S. Amateur. Young's career at the club spanned eight decades, and he is a member of the inaugural class of the PCA Worldwide Caddie Hall of Fame.

(Photo courtesy of Saucon Valley Country Club)

William "Dynamite" Goodloe Jr. (left) and Jim McHale Jr. discuss strategy during the 1949 Walker Cup Matches at the Winged Foot Golf Club in Mamaroneck, New York.

(Photo courtesy of Saucon Valley Country Club)

Pre-tournament favorite Frank Stranahan blasts from the greenside bunker on the 18th hole of his first round match against Robert Kuntz. Kuntz would birdie the 17th and 18th holes to square the match, and eventually defeat Stranahan on the 20th hole.

(Photo courtesy of Saucon Valley Country Club)

Arnold Blum of Macon, Georgia, chips from behind the 18th green in his quarter-final match versus Billy Maxwell. Blum failed to save par and would eventually lose on the 20th hole.

(Photo courtesy of Saucon Valley Country Club)

Saucon Valley member Jim McHale Jr. (right) congratulates Billy Joe Patton after Patton's 1 up victory in their third round match.

(Photo courtesy of Saucon Valley Country Club)

Semi-finalists pose with the Havemeyer Trophy. (Left to right) Joe Gagliardi, Billy Maxwell, Tommy Jacobs, John Benson.

(Photo courtesy of Saucon Valley Country Club)

The scene around the 14th green following Maxwell's hole-out from the bunker during the morning round of the finals versus Joe Gagliardi. On the right side of the photo Maxwell can been seen walking off the green.

(Photo courtesy of Saucon Valley Country Club)

Bill Stern of NBC radio congratulates Billy Maxwell immediately following his victory in the 1951 U.S. Amateur Championship. Stern's interview of Maxwell would broadcast live to a national audience.

(Photo courtesy of Saucon Valley Country Club)

'Maxwell Wins National Amateur' headline story.
(Image courtesy of *The Odessa American*)

(From left to right) Eugene Grace, Billy Maxwell, and USGA President James Standish with the Havemeyer Trophy.
(Photo courtesy of Saucon Valley Country Club)

A crowd of over 1,000 remained for the awards ceremony held at the pool area. This view shows the large crowd with the clubhouse in the background.
(Photo courtesy of Saucon Valley Country Club)

A massive gallery follows play on the 15th fairway during the morning round of the finals. All existing attendance records for the U.S. Amateur were broken at Saucon Valley in 1951.
(Photo courtesy of Saucon Valley Country Club)

Located at the first tee of the Old Course, this plaque commemorates all champions of USGA championships held at Saucon Valley. To date, the club has played host to seven USGA championships the 1951 U.S. Amateur being the first.
(author photo)

(From left to right) William Gordon, Eugene Grace, and V.J. "Pat" Pazzetti. Gordon would go on to design both the Grace and Weyhill courses at Saucon Valley under the watchful eye of Pazzetti, long-time Green Committee Chairman.
(Photo courtesy of Saucon Valley Country Club)

The Saucon Valley Country Club "brain trust," (from left to right) W.H. Johnstone, V.J. Pazzetti, Eugene Grace, Norborne Berkeley, R.H. Schlottman, and John J. Somerville.
(Photo courtesy of Saucon Valley Country Club)

Billy Maxwell meets with members of the press following his 4 & 3 triumph over Joe Gagliardi in the final match of the 1951 U.S. Amateur Championship.

(Photo courtesy of Saucon Valley Country Club)

"Giant Killer of Winged Foot" versus "The West Texas Cyclone." Joe Gagliardi (left) and Billy Maxwell pose for this photograph prior to the final match of the 51st U.S. Amateur Championship.

(Photo courtesy of Saucon Valley Country Club)

USGA President James Standish congratulates newly crowned U.S. Amateur champion Billy Maxwell.

(Photo courtesy of Saucon Valley Country Club)

1951 U.S. Amateur Championship Contestants

-A-

Addington, Don Dallas, Texas
Ahern, Randall R. Northville, Michigan
Albertus, Robert Wallingford, Pennsylvania
Alexander, Dr. William H. Petersburg, Virginia
Allan, Francis J. West Pittston, Pennsylvania
Allman, Richard Philmont, Pennsylvania
Andzel, Walter C. Hamburg, New York

-B-

Babbish, Robert N. Detroit, Michigan
Ballard, Dempsey E. Wichita Falls, Texas
Barnes, Thomas W. Atlanta, Georgia
Battle, John S., Jr. Charlottesville, Virginia
Benson, J.C. Pittsburgh, Pennsylvania
Beyer, H. Lloyd, Jr. Newtown Square, Pennsylvania
Bishop, Stanley E. Weston, Massachusetts
Bisplinghoff, Donald Orlando, Florida
Blair, James T., III Overland Park, Kansas
Blanton, William D. Greensboro, North Carolina
Blum, Arnold Macon, Georgia
Boatwright, P.J., Jr. Spartanburg, South Carolina
Brewer, Gay, Jr. Lexington, Kentucky
Brown, J. Wolcott Brielle, New Jersey
Brownell, Robert W. Chevy Chase, Maryland
Brownlow, George W., Jr. Wilson, North Carolina

-C-

Calder, Stanley Montclair, New Jersey
Cameron, John N.C. Houston, Texas
Campbell, Keith Logansport, Indiana
Campbell, William C. Huntington, West Virginia
Cardinal, Robert J. San Francisco, California

Carey, Emerson, III Denver, Colorado
Carey, Emerson, Jr. Denver, Colorado
Carey, William, Jr. Denver, Colorado
Chandler, Robert P. Landover, Maryland
Chapin, William C. Rochester, New York
Chapman, Richard D. Pinehurst, North Carolina
Cisco, Walter Louisville, Kentucky
Coe, Charles R. Oklahoma City, Oklahoma
Collord, I. Richard, Jr. New Orleans, Louisiana
Connolly, Frank Mount Clemens, Michigan
Crannell, L.M., Jr. Dallas, Texas
Creason, Lynn A. Harrisburg, Pennsylvania
Cross, Harold S., Jr. Philadelphia, Pennsylvania

-D-

Dana, Lawrence, Jr. Greensburg, Pennsylvania
Dawson, George Mamaroneck, New York
Dawson, John W. Hollywood, California
Dennis, David B. Independence, Kansas
Dorsett, A.D., Jr. Salisbury, North Carolina
Dudlik, Mike Johnson City, New York
Dudley, Charles B. Greenville, South Carolina

-E-

Ebbers, Harold L. Clearwater, Florida
Eckis, Robert E., Jr. Williamsville, New York
Emanuelson, Herbert L., Jr. Orange, Connecticut
Emery, Walter Tulsa, Oklahoma
Ervasti, Edward Normandy, Missouri
Evans, Charles, Jr. Chicago, Illinois
Evans, Richard E. Cleveland, Ohio
Everitt, Howard Northfield, New Jersey

-F-

Ferrie, James Long Beach, California
Finsterwald, Dow Athens, Ohio
Frisina, James Springfield, Illinois

-G-

Gagliardi, Joseph F. Mamaroneck, New York
Gardner, Robert Los Angeles, California
Giddings, Richard J. Modesto, California
Goldwater, Robert Phoenix, Arizona
Goodes, Benny Greensboro, North Carolina
Gordon, Kenneth T. Montclair, New Jersey
Guariglia, Donald R. St. Louis, Missouri

-H-

Harison, William M., Jr. Augusta, Georgia
Harrington, George Medford, Oregon
Harrington, Paul R. Houston, Texas
Harrington, Robert C. Frederick, Maryland
Harrison, Charles W. Atlanta, Georgia
Haverstick, H.H., Jr. Lancaster, Pennsylvania
Healey, James T. Orange, Connecticut
Heller, Leo Malvern, Pennsylvania
Hoffman, Larry Reno, Pennsylvania
Hogan, Royal Fort Worth, Texas
Holland, Tim Rockville Centre, New York
Holscher, Frank Pacific Palisades, California
Hopkins, Edwin B., Jr. Abilene, Texas
Howard, Alan Davenport, Iowa
Humm, John J. Rockville Centre, New York
Humphrey, Dudley S. Cleveland, Ohio
Hyndman, William, III Abington, Pennsylvania

-J-

Jackson, James G. Kirkwood, Missouri
Jacobs, K. Tommy, Jr. Montebello, California
Jamison, Thomas S., Jr. Greensburg, Pennsylvania
Janssen, Benno, Jr. Charlottesville, Virgina
Jaros, Michael Endicott, New York
Jennings, Richard A. Lubbock, Texas
Johnston, Edward A. Towson, Maryland

-K-

Key, Billy Columbus, Georgia
Kirkpatrick, Harreld N. Owensboro, Kentucky
Knowles, Robert W., Jr. Brookline, Massachusetts
Kosten, Robert T. Omaha, Nebraska
Kowal, Henry J. Poughkeepsie, New York
Kowal, Stanley Albany, New York
Kringle, Edward Sacramento, California
Kuntz, Robert W. Larchmont, New York

L-

Lee, James M., Jr. Tallahassee, Florida
Lees, William P. Portland, Oregon
Leonard, Thomas J., Jr. Nashua, New Hampshire
Loeb, Allan M. Glencoe, Illinois
Lostoski, Louis C. Bristol, Connecticut

-M-

Malloy, Jack Oklahoma City, Oklahoma
Manley, Hobart L., Jr. Savannah, Georgia
Martin, Edward P. Winchester, Massachusetts
Martz, Lloyd A. Royal Oak, Michigan
Mawhinney, William C. Vancouver, B.C.
Maxwell, Billy Odessa, Texas
McArdle, Francis Wayland, Massachusetts

McBride, Joseph A. Ridgewood, New Jersey
McCreary, Richard E., Jr. Houston, Texas
McCullough, W.B., Jr. Abington, Pennsylvania
McHale, James B., Jr. Bethlehem, Pennsylvania
Meister, Edward I., Jr. Willoughby, Ohio
Michalek, Frank Baltimore, Maryland
Miller, Clancy St. Joseph, Missouri
Morano, Dom Englewood, New Jersey
Morey, Dale Martinsville, Indiana
Morine, Kenneth H. Highland Park, Illinois
Moseley, Capt. Frederick G. San Antonio, Texas
Moynihan, John L., Jr. Albany, New York
Mucci, Pat Paterson, New Jersey
Munger, Jack R. Dallas, Texas

-N-

Nauts, Richard L. Houston, Texas
Neese, L.E., Jr. Burlington, North Carolina

-O-

Oatman, Glenn A. Independence, Missouri
O'Connor, Frank E., Jr. East Amherst, New York
Olfs, Arthur C., Jr. Birmingham, Michigan
Oliver, Joseph W. Pittsburgh, Pennsylvania
Olson, Robert Grosse Pointe Woods, Michigan
Owens, John C. Lexington, Kentucky
Ozol, Rudolph J. Union, New Jersey

-P-

Paddock, Harold D., Jr. Aurora, Ohio
Panowski, Dr. Walter J. Towson, Maryland
Patton, William J. Morganton, North Carolina
Paul, James W. Locust Valley, New York
Peck, Jack R. Logan, West Virginia

Person, Curtis Memphis, Tennessee
Peterson, Arthur Fitchburg, Massachusetts
Picard, William H. Charleston, South Carolina
Pierce, Thomas M. Rutland, Vermont
Pincus, David Elkins Park, Pennsylvania
Price, Charles B. Bethesda, Maryland

-Q-

Quinn, Cameron P. Rumford, Rhode Island
Quinn, John J. Baltimore, Maryland

-R-

Rendleman, Richard J. Salisbury, North Carolina
Ribner, Lloyd D. White Plains, New York
Riegel, Robert F. Beaumont, Texas
Robinson, William J. Philadelphia, Pennsylvania
Rogers, Ken Oklahoma City, Oklahoma

-S-

Sanok, Chester Upper Montclair, New Jersey
Schwab, Ralph G. Dayton, Ohio
Selby, John H. Dallas, Texas
Semple, Harton S. Sewickley, Pennsylvania
Sheehan, Thomas E. Birmingham, Michigan
Sheldon, Charles Miami Beach, Florida
Shepherd, Joel M. Richland, Michigan
Shields, William Albany, New York
Simonsen, Ade Minneapolis, Minnesota
Sixty, Billy, Jr. Wauwatosa, Wisconsin
Souchak, Frank S., Jr. Oakmont, Pennsylvania
Spencer, Wynsol K. Newport News, Virginia
Stalls, Bill Greenville, North Carolina
Stanley, Dave Montebello, California
Stembler, W.Y. Miami, Florida
Stephens, Richard A. Newtown Square, Pennsylvania

Stewart, Jack Phoenix, Arizona
Strack, Charles York, Pennsylvania
Strafaci, Frank Garden City, New York
Stranahan, Frank R. Toledo, Ohio
Strange, Tom, Jr. Cincinnati, Ohio
Studinger, George San Francisco, California

-T-

Taylor, Ellis Newark, Delaware
Taylor, Leon Tyler, Texas
Taylor, Perry T. Huntington, West Virginia
Taylor, Ray H., Jr. Pinehurst, North Carolina
Torgerson, Reinert M. Garden City, New York
Trainor, Dr. George M. Pittsford, New York
Turnesa, William P. Elmsford, New York
Tutwiler, E.M., Jr. Oak Hill, West Virginia

-U-

Urzetta, Sam Rochester, New York

-V-

Venturi, Kenneth San Francisco, California
Victor, George E. Golf, Illinois

-W-

Wagner, John E. Glencoe, Illinois
Walker, Delbert Long Beach, California
Ward, Harvie, Jr. Fayetteville, North Carolina
Ward, John P. Clay, New York
Weaver, John Houston, Texas
Welch, Harry Salisbury, North Carolina
Welsh, Alex Rockford, Illinois
Weston, Raymond E., Jr. Spokane, Washington

Wild, Claude C., Jr. Arlington, Virginia
Wilke, Robert E. Noroton, Connecticut
Wininger, Francis G. Northfield, New Jersey
Wittenberg, James A. Memphis, Tennessee

-Y-

Young, Sanford Greensboro, North Carolina

-Z-

Zinn, Jack Royal Oak, Michigan
Zuspann, Eugene P. Goodland, Kansas

Billy Maxwell
Career Victories

Amateur Record

U.S. Amateur, 1951
Runner-up: Joe Gagliardi 4 & 3

Mexican Amateur, 1953
Runner-up: Frank Stranahan 8 & 7

Professional Record

Azalea Open, 1955
(65-68-68-69=270) Runner-up: Mike Souchak

Mexican Open, 1956
(264, record score) Runner-up: Roberto DeVicenzo

Arlington Open, 1956
(64-69-70-69=272) Runner-up: George Bayer, Ernie Vossler (273)

Hesperia Open Invitatonal, 1957
(67-67-67-74=275) Runner-up: Dow Finsterwald (277)

Memphis Open, 1958
(69-65-68-65=267) Runner-up: Cary Middlecoff (268)

Puerto Rico Open, 1961

Palm Springs (Bob Hope) Classic, 1961
(68-70-68-68-71=345) Runner-up: Doug Sanders (347)

Insurance City Open Invitational, 1961
(69-68-68-66=271) Runner-up: Ted Kroll (Playoff)

Dallas Open Invitatonal (Byron Nelson Classic), 1962
(68-70-68-71=277) Runner-up: Johnny Pott (281)

Florida Open, 1973

Billy Maxwell
Record in Major Championships

Amateur Record

Masters – *Augusta National Golf Club, Augusta, Georgia*
T-49, 1952

U.S. Amateur Championship
R16, 1950 – Minneapolis Golf Club, St. Louis Park, Minnesota
1, 1951 – Saucon Valley Country Club, Bethlehem, Pennsylvania
R256, 1952 – Seattle Golf Club, Seattle, Washington

The Amateur Championship (British Amateur)
R16, 1952 – Prestwick Golf Club, South Ayrshire, Scotland

Professional Record

Masters – *Augusta National Golf Club, Augusta, Georgia*
T-43, 1954
T-18, 1955
T-34, 1956
WD, 1957
T-9, 1958
T-8, 1959
T-25, 1960
T-5, 1962
T-15, 1963
T-18, 1964
T-26, 1965
T-39, 1966

U.S. Open Championship

27, 1955 - Olympic Club (Lake Course), San Francisco, California

12, 1956 - Oak Hill Country Club (East Course), Rochester, New York

T-8, 1957 - Inverness Club, Toledo, Ohio

T-27, 1958 - Southern Hills Country Club, Tulsa, Oklahoma

T-26, 1959 -Winged Foot Golf Club (West Course), Mamaroneck, New York

T-22, 1961 - Oakland Hills Country Club (South Course), Bloomfield Hills, Michigan

T-8, 1962 - Oakmont Country Club, Oakmont, Pennsylvania

T-5, 1963 - The Country Club (Composite Course), Brookline, Massachusetts

14, 1965 - Bellerive Country Club, St. Louis, Missouri

T-36, 1966 – Olympic Club (Lake Course), San Francisco, California

PGA Championship

T-25, 1958 - Llanerch Country Club, Havertown, Pennsylvania

T-11, 1959 - Minneapolis Golf Club, St. Louis Park, Minnesota

T-24, 1960 - Firestone Country Club (South Course), Akron, Ohio

T-27, 1961 - Olympia Fields Country Club, Olympia Fields, Illinois

WD, 1962 - Aronimink Golf Club, Newtown Square, Pennsylvania

T-5, 1963 - Dallas Athletic Club (Blue Course), Dallas, Texas

T-13, 1964 - Columbus Country Club, Columbus, Ohio

T-43, 1965 - Laurel Valley Golf Club, Ligonier, Pennsylvania

T-63, 1969 - NCR Country Club (South Course), Dayton, Ohio

T-10, 1970 - Southern Hills Country Club, Tulsa, Oklahoma

T-40, 1971 - PGA National Golf Club, Palm Beach Gardens, Florida

The Open Championship (British Open)

DNP

WD = Withdrew from competition
"T" indicates tie for a place
R256, R128, R64, R32, R16, QF, SF = Round in which player lost in match play
DNP = Did not play

Billy Maxwell
Record in Ryder Cup Competiton

1963 – Atlanta Athletic Club, Atlanta, Georgia

United States 23 - Great Britain & Ireland 9

Foursomes

Billy Maxwell and Bob Goalby def. Dave Thomas and Harry Weetman 4 & 3

Four-Ball

Billy Maxwell and Billy Casper def. Harry Weetman and George Will 3 & 2

Billy Maxwell and Billy Casper def. Tom Haliburton and Geoffrey Hunt 1 up

Singles

Billy Maxwell def. Christy O'Connor 2 & 1

Billy Maxwell Ryder Cup Record: 4-0-0

Edwards Brothers Malloy
Thorofare, NJ USA
April 21, 2016